BISON
BOOKS

River Teeth Literary Nonfiction Prize

SERIES EDITORS:
Daniel Lehman, Ashland University
Joe Mackall, Ashland University

The River Teeth Literary Nonfiction Prize is
awarded to the best work of literary nonfiction
submitted to the annual contest sponsored by
River Teeth: A Journal of Nonfiction Narrative.

Mountains
of Light

Seasons of Reflection in Yosemite

R. MARK LIEBENOW

University of Nebraska Press: Lincoln and London

An essay titled "Hiking Over the Edge"
came from parts of two chapters in this
book. The essay won the Chautauqua
Nonfiction Prize and was published in
the *Chautauqua Literary Journal* in 2011.
© 2011 Mark Liebenow, reprinted by
permission of *Chautauqua*.

Library of Congress
Cataloging-in-Publication Data

Liebenow, R. Mark
(Ronald Mark), 1953–
Mountains of light: seasons of reflection
in Yosemite / R. Mark Liebenow.
p. cm. —(River Teeth Literary
Nonfiction Prize)
ISBN 978-0-8032-4017-9
(pbk.: alk. paper)
I. Title.
PS3612.I328M68 2012
811'.6—dc23
2011035846

Set in Arno Pro by Bob Reitz.
Designed by Ashley Muehlbauer.

To Evelyn MacNair,
who pushed me to go camping
whenever I began to drive her crazy

Contents

Acknowledgments

I am thankful to Jim Hicks, who first took me to Yosemite, and to Molly and Francesco Cassford-Curcio, who encouraged me to go further in my writing. Steve Cary, Daniel Pryfogle, John Westlake, and Thomas Palakeel read parts of my adventures and offered invaluable insights. Emily Nelms's careful editing helped create order out of my trail notes, and Marlene Gabriel believed in this manuscript in its early stages and shared her encouragement. My gratitude also goes to John Muir, whose life and words have challenged me to listen more closely to nature.

Mountains of Light

Entering the Wilderness

There . . . rises a majestic forest of Silver Fir blooming in eternal freshness, and the snow beneath the trees strewn with their beautiful plumes.

—John Muir, *Mountains of California*

Cocooned in my down sleeping bag, I listen to the darkness. What am I doing here, John? Why do I seek your "eternal freshness?"

In the middle of the night something pushes on my toes. Half asleep, I think a nocturnal squirrel is rooting around at the bottom of my tent. There is scuffling and the animal bumps hard against the hollows of my feet. That's no squirrel. It's larger, perhaps a raccoon. Then I hear a low guttural snort and *National Geographic* images rush into my head—grizzlies mauling their helpless prey, wolves tearing elk apart with their long savage teeth.

With my heart pounding, I lie as still as a mummy.

When I hear the creature shuffle away, I risk sitting up, making as little noise as possible, and peek out the tent's opening.

I detect a sour musky scent but the darkness is so thick that at first I don't see anything. Then the animal moves into the slight moonlight hovering between trees a dozen feet away and I'm able to make out a back that is big, black, and shaggy.

Bears unsettle me when they are this close. They are strong enough to rip the doors off cars when hungry, can flatten a tent in one leap, and have claws that can shred the bark of trees. My shelter's thin nylon skin wouldn't stop a chipmunk determined to get in. It's January and this bear is supposed to be hibernating, not roaming around.

Pulling my head back in, I zip up the tent and force myself to lie down. I listen to the sounds of the wilderness for a long time, hear the twitching of branches and the rustling of dry leaves. I do not sleep well.

At 6:30 a.m., tired from conjuring danger from every stray noise and stiff from sleeping on the ground, I pull on clothes that froze overnight and step gingerly into the darkness, cautious of wild animals still prowling around. Leidig Meadow and the Merced River, whose waters sing nearby, are barely visible in the predawn light of the young moon. Night hides the canyon walls under a cloak of blackness while overhead thousands of sparkling, spinning stars, scattered like seeds across the infinite of the universe, dance in the dark silence that surrounds the earth. Into this wonder rises the crisp beauty of dawn, a narrow orange band of light that pierces the eastern horizon. The mountain's scent condenses on my upturned face as I breathe in the valley and its peacefulness, then slowly exhale. My breath rises straight up in the still air.

As daylight floods over the mountains, the grandeur of Yosemite emerges and surrounds me with rivers, waterfalls, forests, and sky. The fresh pine air quickens my pulse. I do not know where

I am going now that I'm here, but I know this is the beginning of something that has been waiting.

Yosemite Valley is seven miles long, one mile wide, and ringed by vertical walls a mile high. In winter the smells on the breeze are simple and direct—earth, granite, cedar, and oak. Most of Yosemite's waterfalls are quiet. They spout water over the stone cliffs rather than roar with the rush of the spring cascades. One hundred feet in front of me, a doe and two of her offspring meander around each other in slow measured steps, eating acorns on the ground. In this season of bare sounds the silver Merced River trickles over dark brown, ice-covered stones and through emerald pools that line the shallows as the river flows down the middle of the valley. A red-tailed hawk flies overhead, checking for food. On the left, beyond the deer, the spray of water flowing over Yosemite Falls freezes into a shower of sparkling crystals. Wisps of snow fog hover a foot over the meadow, and groves of dark green pine trees stand mute, waiting for the sun's warmth.

On the south side of the valley, massive Sentinel Rock rises like a gray tower over the meadow at its feet. The Four Mile Trail begins there, at the base of Sentinel, and zigzags up under the trees that cling to the steep granite wall on its way to Glacier Point. Closed now because of snow, the trail leads to granite peaks that catch the first rays of the still-hidden sun and shine as beacons of light. Five hundred feet away on my right, out in the meadow, a coyote pokes holes in the snow with its nose, tilting its head to hear mice skittering beneath, then pouncing on their snow tunnels. On the far side of the river a second coyote trots purposely along the road, heading somewhere. Ravens call to each other across the emptiness with slow, thoughtful caws. Their echoes haunt the thinness of the air.

❧

I've been coming to Yosemite for a number of years, hiking the trails around the valley and soaking up the scenery. I feel alive when I'm here, smelling the clean air and drinking the fresh water, listening to birds happily chatter away in the trees. The simple beauty of the forests, rivers, and granite mountains reaching into blue sky tell me that I am part of something much greater than my life. I come here to be inspired, to regroup from the fraying activities of work. I sleep on the ground, cook simple meals, hike through the hours of the day, and come back at night to sleep. I am comfortable in the valley, yet still a visitor. A week after returning to the city I feel the pull to come back because something special is here, and I want to know what it is.

There is another reason why I have come to the valley. My wife, Evelyn, recently died of a heart condition that we never knew she had. She was a teacher of the learning challenged, a talented singer, and a defender of orphans and abandoned pets. Because she died so young (in her forties), my friends don't know what to say to help. Her death devastated me, and I have been struggling, unsure what I do with my life now. So I have come to listen for nature's wisdom. In the past, the valley has helped me face my problems, see more clearly what was going on and what needed to be done. I'm not an emotionally expressive person, and I fear that if I do not face grief directly, it will tear me apart inside.

People have long traveled to the wilderness to clear their minds and focus their hearts—the prophets, Jesus, Mohammad, the Desert Fathers and Mothers, Buddha. Business leaders come, as do housewives and truckers needing to get away. Also poets and musicians, like my friend Shira, who takes her violin to the Grand Canyon to compose. People need to feel the presence of something greater than their lives if they are to flourish. They need to be inspired, and Yosemite does this for me.

As soon as I enter the valley I roll the windows down and the sounds of the river and the pine smells of Yosemite pour in. My senses perk up as if I have entered a magical world or a circle has been completed by my return. The heaviness of life falls off as the light of the wilderness warms my face and radiates in. Gradually I relax, forget about the work I have to do when I get home, and slow my pace.

In the twenty-nine-degree air I pull my stocking cap down for an extra inch of warmth, and glance behind to see if any animals are sneaking up, having taken exception to my presence. This is their world, not mine. In the city I'm the one in control. The sun rises and sets to the flick of an electric switch. The river flows through pipes with the turn of a faucet. Heat and cooling are available to keep me comfortable. When camping, I put myself at the mercy of the elements. When the weather is cold or rainy, humid or sweltering, so am I. Shelter, water, and food are not available on a hike if a storm sweeps in and I haven't planned ahead. And often enough pieces of the valley wall break off, completely indifferent to my plans, and take out the trail I need to use to get down into the valley and back to camp.

I want to stop being a visitor and move deeper into this place, see beneath the valley's beauty that surprises me at every turn. Not knowing how to accomplish this, I kneel where I am and look closely at the milkweed plant in front of me. I try to see the line where domesticity ends and wildness begins, wanting to know what makes it different from its cousin in the city. A delicate layer of frost has crystallized on the upper surface of its purple and green mottled leaves, transforming them into finely crafted glass. I would not have noticed them had I kept on walking.

On the other side of the meadow coyotes start yipping. I hurry over, thrilled to see something more energetic than the bucolic deer, but when I arrive the coyotes are gone. I run to the next meadow just in time to see them trot out the other side. The sun rises above the mountains and shoots long streamers of light over the snow-hooded top of Half Dome, setting Eagle Peak on fire five thousand feet above me. This light slowly burns down the north wall to the valley floor until all the rocks and trees are aflame with dawn's yellow. I head for a warm breakfast.

The cafeteria is scattered with early risers, mostly older folks who are staying in the climate-controlled lodge but also a few people like me, who are camping in the snow and want a place to warm up. Rock climbers have piled layers of coats on the chairs around them as they flip through climbing maps, trying to decide which routes they'll attempt. Dishes and utensils clatter as we pick from a choice of bacon, pancakes, eggs, cold cereals, oatmeal, bagels, toast, and yogurt. I choose what I think the pioneers ate: eggs, sausage, biscuits and gravy. The latter turns out to be a mistake. The eggs and sausage would have been enough on their own, but the biscuits and gravy are heavy. Each forkful loads my stomach lower, like cement blocks being added to the back of a pickup truck. I feel like the snake in the *Far Side* cartoon that has swallowed a person whole, and whose outline is still visible standing up in the snake's stomach. The snake says something like, "Should I have chewed?" But I dutifully eat everything because I can't waste food, then waddle outside to walk around, hoping I don't have to bend for a couple of hours.

The people I've read about in the history books are gone, and much of what they built has been absorbed back into the land. The pioneers have long been dead, and the Native culture exists only during the warm months when tribal experts like Julia and Lucy

Parker drive in to demonstrate Native crafts. On the historical marker signs posted around the reconstructed Indian village are descriptions of how the Natives lived in harmony with what the environment provided naturally, how their acorn granaries—the low-tech elevated bins constructed of bark and grass—preserved food for two years in case of a poor harvest, and how their population quickly declined when the pioneers moved in.

THE AHWAHNECHEES

Native Americans began living in Yosemite four thousand years ago. In the early 1800s Chief Teneiya formed his band out of individuals from area tribes and moved them to the valley called Ahwahnee. He named his group the "Yosemite" (Grizzly Bear).

When Europeans arrived in the 1850s, 250 Ahwahnechees were living in the area. They had nine camps in the valley, with the main one near the base of Yosemite Falls. Winter huts were conical and used poles covered by the bark of trees. Religious ceremonies were elaborate and highly symbolic.

Black oak acorns made up 60 percent of the Ahwahnechees' diet, and each family of four ate five hundred pounds of acorns a year. The Ahwahnechees regularly set forest fires to increase oak production. They hunted deer, quail, and grouse, fished for mountain trout, and traded with area tribes like the Mono Lake Paiutes and the Sierra Miwoks. Many plants were used in daily life.

From the middle of the Native village, Yosemite Falls is visible through an opening in the trees. A shift in the wind has blown the fall's meager spray against the valley wall, where it has frozen in a thousand-foot splash of white, like a frosted image of a Native American leader. I imagine that when the early people saw this happen, the result moved beyond being frozen water to speaking of deeper things, of connections between the spirits of ancestors and the tribe's daily life, of messages sent from the other world to guide them.

Quiet permeates the village today because no Ahwahnechees have lived here for more than a century, although their descendants still use the roundhouse and sweathouse for religious ceremonies—dancing, prayer, and purification. Both conical structures were built deep into the ground to connect them to Mother Earth; only the brown cedar bark roofs are still visible. The smoke hole in the roof of the roundhouse connected the people to the spirits in the sky. The whirling dervishes of Sufi Islam have a similar awareness, and when they dance they spin with one hand down to honor the earth and the other hand open toward heaven. In the center of the roundhouse is the charred remains of a fire. A beam of sunlight comes through the hole in the roof into the shadows where Chief Teneiya once sat and discussed tribal matters with elders in the circle.

Further on is a flat granite rock with several round holes worn into it where acorns were ground to make meal, as well as the place where the Ahwahnechees skinned deer and used the hides, bones, and sinews to make clothing. Under this tree they gathered their children and passed on stories of ancient wisdom from the ancestors. Here they slept in teepees. Here they harvested manzanita berries to make tea. Listening for what they likely heard, I hear the sound of the falls grow louder, then softer, then louder again in a rhythm that hesitates like an afterthought. I touch the surface of the creek to check the temperature, curious as to why something so shallow hasn't frozen. My hand feels a pulse, as if the flow of Yosemite Falls can be felt all the way over here, throbbing through the creek like a capillary from the deep heart of the mountain.

Across the road, the Pioneer Cemetery has graves of children laid out beside adults, white settlers alongside Natives, and a few graves without names. The epitaphs on the headstones reveal the dangers present to their lives: some of them were swept over waterfalls, died of various illnesses, or had a horse fall on them, which apparently was a common problem. One grave is Sadie Schaeffer's, who grew up seven miles north of John Muir's home in Wisconsin, thirty miles from Aldo Leopold's Sand County and forty miles from my hometown near Madison. Fourteen years old, she drowned in the river by El Capitan. Friends wrote on her tombstone, "Ah, that beauteous head . . . it carried sunshine into the rapids."

A number of the valley's early historical people are here, too. Galen Clark came to these mountains ill in 1855, expecting to die, but regained his health because of the air, he said, and lived fifty more years. His grave is framed by the four redwoods he planted in anticipation. He became Yosemite's first guardian and built a cabin among the giant sequoias of the Mariposa Grove. James Hutchings, the editor of a national magazine, is buried in the corner. One of the valley's first tourists, he found it hard to leave because nothing back in society compared to this, and he made it his life's work to let Yosemite's wonders be known. J. C. Lamon rests in the middle. He was the first settler to stay in the valley year round and he planted the apple orchard that still exists by Curry Village.

At Degnan's Deli, a convenience store set up in the wilderness, I pick up coffee and talk with Diane, who is often working the register. With the emptiness of the house back home, it is enticing to think of moving here, of leaving everything behind, especially the noise and rush of city life, and starting over. My community would be among others who came because of what they found in nature here or because of what they wanted to leave behind. Our needs would be simple and relationships guided by the changing seasons. We would rise with the sun and gather in the evening to share our stories of the wonders we had seen. My hope is that being here for a week will slow down my incessant drive to accomplish things.

I'm sleeping in Camp 4 (also known as Sunnyside) where the rock climbers stay. There aren't many climbers now, perhaps thirty, judging by the number of tents, and it's been a mild winter. I chat with Tom and Gerold, from Australia, as they eat breakfast, and ask where they're climbing today. "Anywhere in the sun!" they mutter, hands wrapped around the metal coffeepot heating on the fire. I keep moving in the chilled air and follow the trail along the northern edge of the valley floor. Half a mile down, climbers on Rixon's Pinnacle are learning to set safety gear into the five-hundred-foot column of rock in case they lose their grip on the sheer granite wall and fall. There's also an enormous band of glacial scraping, where rocks embedded in the side of a glacier scratched horizontal grooves hundreds of feet long into the valley wall. The grooves are at least ten thousand years old, which is when the last glacier came through and carved the original "v" shape of the valley into a "u." The passing years have scarcely dulled the marks.

Eighty feet to the side, I stretch my arm as far as it will go into a fissure in the wall and feel rock that emerged three million years ago with the first uplift of the Sierra, or perhaps back even further, to 130 million years, when this seabed folded into gentle ridges in the Mesozoic Age. Am I touching the original earth? It's a fanciful thought, yet nothing has disturbed the rock here and I let the possibility linger. The Sierra Nevada is part of the range that reaches north to Alaska and south to Tierra del Fuego at the bottom tip of South America. I imagine I can hear faint echoes of Incas turning rain sticks in the Andes, hoping their showers of cactus needles entice the god of the clouds to share needed rain for crops. I see Inuits in the Arctic, carving totems into the white whale bone of the mythic ancestors who gave birth to their race. In my chest I feel the thump-thump of Yosemite's Natives patiently pounding open and then grinding acorns for food using their heavy granite pestles. The physical strength of these perceptions surprises me and I step back, feeling confronted by the forces that created the world.

Everything here is larger than expected. Yesterday I walked across a small meadow to a two-hundred-foot-tall ponderosa pine, expecting to get there in two minutes. The short walk ended up taking thirty, and when I made it to the tree I couldn't reach up and touch even its lowest branch. I watched a small gray bird, the American dipper (which Muir knew as an ouzel) repeatedly dive into the rapids of a river and bop up and down in the water as if it were dancing. At dawn, sunrise colored the snowy mountains a warm peach color. At the foot of granite domes rising two miles into the air, coyotes tumbled over each other as they played tag. I walked from a blue stream trickling near white-barked aspen to a waterfall cascading two thousand feet, expecting the valley to shout its own praises. But it didn't. There was only a hush that astounded me with its humility.

I feel like I'm walking through a picture postcard. Every direction I turn, another view takes my breath away. It's hard to believe that such a place exists, a place so infused with beauty and majesty that I feel insignificant. Someone on top of Half Dome wouldn't be able to see me standing in the meadow, surrounded as I am by groves of tall trees and valley walls a mile high. Yet that person probably wouldn't be looking into the valley but over the mountain range to the east and watching the sun as it rises over the edge of the earth, sending great yellow beams of light flowing over the crest of dark mountains. One day I will stand up there with my feet above the clouds, and marvel again over the glories of nature.

Half a mile later, at the base of the Lower Brother rock formation, I follow a hunch and turn right onto an indistinct trail that goes under the trees and up a small talus slope. At the top, massive El Capitan rises straight out of the ground at my feet. This is where rock climbers around the world dream of standing. But how does anyone climb up five thousand feet of smooth, vertical rock? There are no handholds or ridges to grasp or stand on. Walking along its side, I finally spot a tiny crack where a metal pin could be slipped in and a rope attached. Pulling themselves up, climbers then might be able to use their fingertips and toes. But it's hard to tell what's above. El Cap is completely vertical; a mile of rock is compressed into a couple inches of my vision. Now the notion that there are distinct routes makes sense; climbers do not just start anywhere. Smiling at my naiveté, I pat El Cap's massive nose as though it's an oversized puppy, head down the talus, and wander toward the south side of the valley. A mile further along the trail, I look back at the trees at the base of El Cap. They look like matchsticks. A couple of red and blue dots are moving halfway up the face of the rock—climbers that were invisible when I was standing beneath them.

In this southwest corner of the valley, Bridalveil Fall is the center of attraction, but in the morning it's still hidden in shadows.

The fall used to be a nice mountain stream that cascaded down to the valley floor. Then the glaciers came through and sheared off the cascades, leaving a six-hundred-foot waterfall. The result of nature's demolition was the creation of a new scene of exquisite beauty out of the remnants of the old. The glaciers also helped form these broad meadows and bring a new generation of life into being. Remnants of those ancient glaciers are still around, higher up in the mountains, waiting for the next ice age to begin. The breeze picks up and mist from the fall swirls out into the air. This gossamer veil soaks me in freezing water and sends me running for cover. The air is also sharply colder on the south side. I begin shivering and jog to warm up, passing the red chapel and crossing the Merced River via Sentinel Bridge. Gratefully I walk back into the sunny warmth of the valley's north side.

Upper Yosemite Falls Hike

In the afternoon I start up the trail that climbs to the top of Yosemite Falls, layered against the cold but not really knowing what to expect. It's one of the shorter hikes and it's the only trail going up a canyon wall that the park rangers believe is open all the way to the top. After ten minutes of moving briskly up steep switchbacks, I'm too warm and take my jacket off, stuffing it into my backpack. Five minutes later the sweater comes off. I slow the pace even more because my legs begin to cramp and I have to catch my breath. When I reach the Columbia Rock overlook, a thousand feet above the valley's floor, I take a break and massage my legs. The entire valley is laid out before me in a panorama—North Dome, Half Dome, Glacier Point, Sentinel Rock, and Taft Point. Three waterfalls flow over valley walls dusted with snow, and the dark Merced River winds its way through the length of the white meadows. I notice dark gray clouds on the horizon, either sliding by to the south or moving in, I can't tell which. I debate whether to head down as a precaution, but I can't let go of the view, captivated by the scene developing in front of me. I'll go on, I tell myself, and turn back if the storm moves closer.

Two hours later I reach the top of the valley wall, clean snow off a flat rock, and collapse. The trail is only three miles long but it also goes up a mile in elevation and I'm not in shape. The entire Sierra range looks raw, as if the glaciers had scrubbed the dark mountains down to bare stone. John Muir and I didn't see anything like this during our childhoods in the gentle hills of Wisconsin. The unsettled, primordial image is stunning.

The Sierra Nevada is a massive granite block that rises three miles into the frozen air and cuts the horizon with a jagged edge. Its wilderness crosses the spine of the mountain range and stretches east to the uninhabited, barren plains of Nevada. The view before me is spectacular and frightening. I can't get a handle on it. If this had been built by humans, I'd be able to figure it out. But this is so different from anything I know. Yosemite is layered in mystery.

The slate-blue flanks of the mountain peaks convey the seriousness of winter in the mountains, yet the valley nestled below is protected from the harshness that permeates the highlands only four thousand vertical feet away. Up here it's ten degrees colder. Hundreds of peaks are scraping snow off the bottom of the heavy, black clouds that are moving relentlessly closer. A gray curtain of falling snow covers the furthest mountains in white. As my body cools down from the hike, sweaters and jackets are layered back on. The wind stops and there are no sounds. Nothing stirs.

Fifty mountain chickadees sweep in out of the sky and fill the bushes around me with a raucous chatter. Then, just as quickly, they are gone, back to foraging for seeds for survival. But in the resulting void of sound, a disturbing thought forms: this is where nature's destructive power lives, where it severs lives with sharp, unforgiving knives. In the midst of these astounding scenes of transcendent beauty, innocent creatures like the chickadees die and nature doesn't seem to care. Bodies fall dead, or are killed, and are quickly eaten. The claws of the owl, the hawk, the coyote close in on the mouse and the squirrel, and there is death. Vultures take the remains away, and tourists like me have no clue about the drama that has gone on.

As the wind dances over the dark-boned wilderness with a soft rasping, slowly wearing away the surface of the land, I feel the truth of Muir's words, that the sounds of nature bring up "multitudes of thoughts and feelings we did not know we possessed." I realize there is no guarantee that anyone or anything will live a long and happy life. There never was, although this was the illusion I accepted until Evelyn's sudden death.

The line between life and death is delicate. Tragic accidents happen, sometimes because of simple inattention. Standing in deep snow in the wilderness at eight thousand feet, I realize that I could easily die today. I feel vulnerable to every calamity I can imagine, and a list begins forming. I could slip, break a leg and freeze to death, because there is no one to notice my absence in time to come looking for me. I could be mauled by a bear, whose paws are as big as my chest, and bleed to death. A mountain lion hiding behind the ridge one hundred feet away could jump on my back and snap my neck in its mouth. Or, if I slipped, I could knock myself unconscious and, once again, freeze to death. I also could slide over the canyon wall like it was a ski jump and be really dead. I'm on the edge of the wilderness where wild animals live on their own terms, like Australian-rules rugby. The meek should not come. The animals here are survivors, having eaten those who were not strong enough or fast enough. In the valley below, our worlds mingle in a blend of wild and tame. Up here, it's their territory. If I get in their way, if I do something stupid, I could be dead in less than an hour.

The weather front has moved closer and is only a few miles away. It's time to head down before a snowstorm strands me here. I walk back to the trail that snakes down the side of the canyon wall and promptly skid on ice along the edge. Picking myself up, I carefully descend the trail, tapping each rock for ice before putting my foot down.

In the evening, hours later, I stir the campfire with a stick, trying to stay awake long enough to sort today's events. Shadows dance with light in the fire's flames. It feels like I walked into the Garden of Eden in winter after Adam and Eve have been kicked out and wild animals are on the loose, wanting their land back. I feel edgy and certain of my mortality. I came here wanting Yosemite to shake me out of my stupor and help me face death. And it has, but it feels like Yosemite wants to do this by having me listen to its stories.

This valley is an ancient place. People have chosen to live here for four thousand years for a reason. Some of these trees were alive when the Egyptians built the pyramids. But the answers I seek go deeper than the scenery. Like looking into the eyes of one's beloved for the first time, I have only glimpsed what moves underneath Yosemite's beauty, what allows it to endure with strength and hope, what gives it such resonant depth. I could get lost in this place for a long time, and that time has begun.

Slowing Down the Mountain

I wish I knew where I was going. Doomed to be "carried of the spirit into wilderness," I suppose.

—John Muir, *Letters to a Friend*

The valley floor has more than one hundred miles of trail that crisscross each other in a number of configurations, especially trails in the eastern end of the valley. Most wind their way over terrain that includes meadows, rivers, and forests. Over the next few days I walk the eastern loop of trails from Camp 4 to Happy Isles to Mirror Lake to Yosemite Village, then go around again so that I can remember each trail, the locations of historical sites, and the unique views that can be taken in. I go around once more taking side trails this time and discovering where they lead. There is no bad trail. Each has its own grand scenery, and the views of the falls, the mountains, and the granite domes keep changing. Eventually I reach the lesser-used paths that snake up the various talus piles and follow the bases of the valley walls, including some paths that fizzle out in bushes and force me to backtrack.

Most mornings I walk the trails that traverse the middle meadows of Leidig, Sentinel, and Cook's to see the wildlife wake to a new day, and walk again at dusk to watch the mountains and the sky change from yellow to crimson to purple.

The trails in the valley west of Camp 4 take a longer commitment of time because they go greater distances with fewer connecting trails, yet they are as full of scenery as everywhere else. The trail to El Capitan that starts at Camp 4 winds through oak woods, then goes around the massive rockslide that fell from Middle Brother some twenty years ago, down to the Merced River with a scenic view of Half Dome, into the meadows lined with aspen trees and 360-degree views, and back into the woods and up the talus to El Cap. In winter and early spring, before leaves fill the trees in the meadows, the entire valley is open to the sky.

Night sets as day rises. Today with the first glimmer of light in the sky I head off on a trail that goes from Curry Village through a still-dark forest to Happy Isles, about half an hour away. Like Henry David Thoreau, I've returned to nature this month to see what Yosemite has to teach by peering under the surface reality of its beauty. Distracted by my expectations of grand discoveries, and haphazardly paying attention in the dark, I get lost.

My asphalt trail has somehow become dirt, and it's overgrown with bushes and fallen limbs. It doesn't look like anyone has walked through here in decades. The dirt path has a wild, rustic look that appeals to my sense of adventure, so I let it lead me deeper into a forest thick with black shadows and a path that is barely visible. When a lighter area appears through the trees on the right, I push through the bushes and walk out at the base of Glacier Point; its peak rises a mile over my head and its massive and glacier-polished slope slides under the land and looks like a giant spatula. Back on the path, I skirt the edge of a fen, step over fallen trees, duck under low-hanging branches, and detour around boulders the size of rooms that have broken off the cliffs overhead and crash-landed at my feet. In a marsh that is probably connected to the fen, an old cabin has sunk two feet into the unstable ground. Gingerly I walk over a crunching mixture of frozen earth and water to look for clues that the early pioneers may have built it, hoping there are no warm springs beneath my feet. The nail heads are round, not square, so it's probably fifty to eighty years old. Back to hiking, and just when I estimate the civilized trail has reached Happy Isles, my path turns into deeper primeval gloom.

The detailed map published by Wilderness Press, which shows every trail and stream and records the land's changing contours in forty-foot increments, does not show a path where I stand. I juggle unsettling thoughts: It's dawn. The caves under these boulders are large and isolated enough to shelter hibernating bears. I'm by myself, even though the rangers cautioned last night that hiking alone was not wise. I walk carefully, trying not to make any sounds. I barely breathe as I tiptoe through the woods. Then I step on a stick that cracks like a gunshot and something explodes at my feet and shoots off through the bushes. I jump back and brace for an attack by a black bear or a mountain lion. When nothing comes hurtling at me to knock me down, I scan the woods to see if any carnivores were awakened by the noise or perhaps angry that I'm traipsing through their bedroom.

Nothing large moves. The California quail come back and settle under the bushes. My heart calms. When I'm reasonably sure that everything else is still asleep, I begin stepping over loose rocks, careful not to disturb any leaves or sticks as I take my eyes off the uneven trail to watch the shadows for movement, anxious to get out as soon as possible. Shaken, I half-seriously expect Hansel and Gretel—abandoned to die in these dark woods, filled with the hideous crones and starving monsters of German myth—to run up and plead with me to lead them out. My indistinct path climbs up yet another rise, slips between a pair of ten-foot boulders, and joins a real trail. The forbidding trail goes to the right into undiluted darkness. I turn left and experience relief when the familiar outskirts of Happy Isles appear up ahead. Crossing the bridge onto the islands, I climb out over rocks and swirling water to the front boulder that splits the river like the prow of a ship. Dawn finally peeks over the top of the canyon wall and squirrels, chipmunks, and hermit thrushes come out to warm in the sun. I try to identify more birds from the guidebook, but few of them look like their pictures and they refuse to hold still.

For half an hour I sit and enjoy the morning's warmth, watching the water cascade down from the highlands. The river shouts on its wild ride toward me. Its whitewater crests jump around like thousands of white rabbits racing each other to the valley floor. When water hits a depression in the riverbed, it swoops down before shooting up into the air with a whoop of delight, and the energy and sounds of all this rushing water overwhelm the quietness of the woods. Here is unbridled joy! Here is true celebration!

It's this exuberance, this wildness, this loud clashing of nature's forces against each other that I desire because living alone back home has become predictable and sedate. Out here survival is a daily battle. Out here is drama and glory, awe and majesty, and there is death. Hiking on any trail, I never know what is waiting around the next bend, yet I feel nature nudging me to put down my agenda and take some risks.

Going into the wilderness after the death of a loved one has been a rite of passage throughout the centuries and across cultures. Only when the past is set aside, one's fears confronted, is the new reality accepted. As Native American boys went on vision quests to become men, so do those who have lost loved ones go on journeys to make the transition to a new world where the deceased never lived nor ever will.

I grew up in the woods and on the lakes of southern Wisconsin. Mountains we didn't have, just bumps on farmland that we proudly called hills. Trees were abundant and I loved to climb them and look into the distance, feeling so at home that I'd fall asleep in their branches. I'd sit on the shore of Rock Lake for hours watching the movement of the clouds and water. I felt physically connected. At the end of winter, when the ice on the lake would break up, the neighborhood boys would pole chunks of ice around like rafts on the Mississippi, pretending we were Huckleberry Finn. In spring we'd climb supple young trees, grab their tops, leap off, and ride them to the ground. Our woods were friendly places, not foreboding like the dark forests of Eastern Europe or the American West, and we harbored few notions of beasts lurking or goblins hiding. There were no wild animals to harm us. There was a lingering sense of the Native Americans who once lived in the area—the Ojibwas, Foxes, and Winnebagos—and, sometimes with Grandpa I found their arrowheads as we walked through plowed fields in the spring. But their memory seemed as distant as the glaciers that came through centuries before, leaving vast moraines and ground-up mountains that became Wisconsin's rich farmlands.

Finding the trail that I should have taken to get here, I walk back to camp with the sounds of the rushing river still ringing in my head.

❧

In the morning, the winter storm that slipped in overnight moves out of the valley, leaving long strands of clouds swirling a hundred feet above the valley floor. New snow covers the trees, hushing the already quiet season. Sunlight gleams hard off the frozen stone of the mountains, and creeks can be heard gurgling all the way across the meadow. This quietness is taking time to adjust to, like walking from the bright, busy streets of San Francisco into the calm shadows of Grace Cathedral. It's almost too quiet. A Douglas squirrel climbs down a tree twenty feet away and does its morning stretches, first one arm, then the other, sticking its bushy tail in the air. I take the hint and slow in my rush to get to the other side of the valley to see if the beauty of the light shining through the trees there is greater than the light shining here. I'm like a child set loose in a candy store, who thinks that the next piece will always taste better, the next view will be even greater. Forcing myself to stay put, I watch the river in Leidig Meadow to see how fast it is flowing and notice a circle rippling over the surface of a side pool that touches a rock and radiates off in a series of circles. I notice little trout swimming under the skin of ice that edges the shore. Thomas Merton, a Catholic monk, wrote that God is shining through the world all the time, but few notice. This is my first intention, to slow down enough to see.

Getting close to the heart of Yosemite is not easy. Every day it feels like I'm standing around at a party I wasn't invited to and the host is nowhere to be seen. I want to feel what Muir felt, the longing that burned at the root of his soul whenever he was called to other duties but every thought continued to tug him back with his love for this wild landscape. I want to ride his avalanche into the valley and feel his ecstasy, cling to the branches at the top of his tree and shout with delight as I'm being tossed back and forth by the gusting winds of a thunderstorm. Standing here I feel thoughtful, lonely, and renewed all at the same time, and questions arise about why. Yet I'm beginning to think that asking questions is part of my problem. I'm trying to control this environment and make it fit into my boxes, like Muir first did when he was collecting and analyzing plant specimens. Questions separate me from nature. It was only after Muir forgot to bring his plant press one day and was forced to watch and listen that he was able to break through and understand how he fit into the outdoors.

Native Americans learned how to exist with nature and for centuries called this valley their home. They honored the animals and birds of earth and passed on wisdom to their children, like how to set a net low over the river to trap ducks, how to play the elder wood whistle during courtship, and how to weave geometrical patterns into their baskets. I see today much the same as what they saw a thousand years ago when they stood on this spot, looked around at the majestic mountains, and watched the Great Spirit walk by in the winter storms. I want to feel their closeness, see the sacredness of their natural world, and hear the Spirit that guided them through the seasons. The spiritual water that flows through this valley nurtured their lives, and I want it to inspire mine.

Late in the afternoon and tired of thinking about the meaning of mountains and trees, I wander through the delta of Yosemite Creek, following a frozen tributary and stumbling over where John Muir's cabin used to stand. A memorial boulder and stone bench mark the location as the cabin long ago fell apart. I sit on the bench, tuck the edges of my coat underneath so my bottom doesn't freeze, and read from Muir's book describing his adventures here: "We are now in the mountains and they are in us, kindling enthusiasm, making every nerve quiver, filling every pore and cell of us." I look up and smile at Yosemite Falls flowing down in front of me, and again when a doe wanders by only ten feet away.

WILDLIFE

Sixty-four million years ago, dinosaurs were on the way out and mammals were beginning to evolve. Two million years ago a major immigration of animals came across the Bering Strait land bridge. Included in this parade were hares, wolves, saber-tooth cats, mammoths, and rodents. For a while, camels and mastodons grazed in the grasslands of the Sierra foothills.

Because of the relatively mild weather all year round, with highs in the eighties in summer and lows in the twenties in winter, the valley maintains a diversity of life. There are 78 species of mammals and 250 species of birds in the park. Among the mammals are black bear, mountain lion, coyote, raccoon, skunk, squirrel, chipmunk, bat, mule deer, and white-footed deer mouse. Numbered among the birds are the Steller's jay, acorn woodpecker, downy woodpecker, robin, Brewer's blackbird, red-shafted flicker, and the American dipper.

In the evening the sun sets and night rises. The granite walls glow with the golden hue of the setting sun. Dinner is chili and corn over the campfire. I cook adequately, but nothing that is worth lingering over. Dessert tonight is one exception. Apple filling is spooned between two pieces of buttered bread in a pie iron, the bread hanging out cut off, and the iron is stuck in the coals to bake. A few minutes later there's hot apple pie. The first one is so tasty and warm that I make another.

Night deepens and time stops as if the hours and minutes have ceased to exist. Time does not move in the night, and those who are awake exist outside the lines of demarcation. Unless the moon is out, the world at 10:00 p.m. looks much as it does at 4:00 a.m. As night thins and dawn approaches, the forces of earth balance the pull of the sun for a moment and all time seems to exist. Then earth takes off its robe of blue shadows and exchanges it for the bright clothes of day. The past particulates back into the earth at the base of trees, and time renews its pace.

Night sets as the day rises. Today the sun and moon rise together like fraternal twins in some kind of celestial synchronicity. The moon always surprises me. Where will it be today, I wonder, peering around trying to predict. Eventually I decide that I have no clue and give up. Then, hearing a sound, I turn around and there's the moon, smiling at me. The Ahwahnechees weren't concerned about predicting the movement of the stars and planets, but they did watch the moon and recognize major constellations. The Milky Way was called "The Ghosts' Road," and events were remembered by lunar notations like "during the harvest moon seven years ago."

Mist Trail—Panorama Trail—Four Mile Trail

At 6:00 a.m. the following day, still snug and warm in my sleeping bag, I decide to take a big risk before I talk myself out of it. In the book I was reading by flashlight last night in the tent, Rick Bass wrote that it's easier to walk your way into a landscape than to think your way in. It's my last full day here this month before I have to return home and I want a physical challenge, something that will test my courage and skill by forcing me to go where it's wild, where I'll have to rely on myself to deal with whatever I encounter in nature. In short, I want the possibility of dying. Climbing friends say that if you can't get hurt then it's not worth the adventure. I throw supplies into the backpack and hurry across the predawn meadows to the path that will take me up to Vernal and Nevada Falls via the Mist Trail, over to Glacier Point on the Panorama Trail, and back into the valley by the Four Mile Trail. Overhead, three stars surround the quarter moon in the dark blue sky. One of the stars is probably Mars, which rose at 1:00 a.m. Venus, Saturn, and Jupiter all set a couple of hours earlier.

The hike will be thirteen miles long with a one-mile gain in elevation. The trail guide says that each of the three trails is deemed a moderate hike in summer, so to attempt all three in winter is a serious challenge, one that might push me beyond my limits. This time I get to Happy Isles using the correct trail, and begin the hike up the Merced Canyon just as the sun sends a shiver of orange streaking along the sky's eastern edge. Officially the trail is closed in winter: the gate is locked across the trail and avalanche warnings are posted. Yet the trail looks okay, so I slip around the gate and promise myself to turn back if conditions get dangerous. Thirty minutes later I reach the icy steps of the Mist Trail, where circles of rainbows dance in the chilled spray thrown up by the water of Vernal Fall that is hitting the rocks below. After Vernal comes the deep-green Emerald Pool, and half an hour of hiking above that I reach Nevada Fall whose river flows behind Half Dome. So far the trail is clear and only a sparse layer of snow covers the ground.

At the top of Nevada I cross back over the Merced River and locate the Panorama Trail on the right, heading to Illilouette Fall. I slowly make my way up another two thousand feet in elevation. Now the seriousness of the season begins. The snow-crusted trail is frozen and runs fifty feet from the edge of a three-thousand-foot drop. Without any trees in the way, the view is spectacular out over the canyon and toward Yosemite Valley in the distance. I caution myself to remember that the trail is never flat and there are no safety railings if I slip.

I descend into a side canyon. Illilouette Creek is at the bottom; its edges are frozen white. A thick blanket of snow covers the other side of the canyon as it rises up to Glacier Point. The bright sun in the sky sparkles on the stream and I sit and listen to the water. The iced tips of low-lying branches, having been dipped into the river like candlesticks by the swaying movement of the breeze, click against each other like glass ornaments. Black rocks along the riverbank are hooded in white snow like Cistercian monks deep in their winter retreat of silence: they chant gabbro prayers as the stream flows by without ceasing, just as it has for centuries. Crossing over, I hike up the snow-blanketed side of the mountain. Most of the time the snow is firm enough to walk over and I sink down only to my ankles. The path shows through now and then and confirms that I'm on a trail going somewhere. Checking the map, it's clear that I need to stay on the right-hand trail since all the left-hand trails lead off into the snow-bound wilderness of the Sierra, where nights are measured by the hours below freezing and I will not survive in my running shoes. Like Muir, I prefer the flexibility of shoes to boots, although with the snow I might be pushing my luck.

The closer I get to Glacier Point, elevation 7,200 feet, the deeper the snow gets and the trail begins to only sporadically show up. I hadn't anticipated this much snow. As a stopgap measure I slip plastic bags over the two layers of socks that are keeping my feet warm. Occasionally I drop into weaker pockets of snow, get swallowed up to my chest, and spend a few anxious moments hauling myself out, wondering how much deeper the snow is going to get and if it would be prudent to turn back. I don't. I push on and in half an hour reach Glacier Point, go to the overhang, look straight down at the valley floor, and feel lightheaded. How is it possible to peer over the sheer edge of a mountain cliff a mile high without being nudged over by a breeze or sucked down by the wonder? From here I could drop a rock straight down onto the dirt path I walked earlier in the week.

Brushing snow off a boulder, I eat lunch overlooking the backcountry where the left-hand trails disappear. The temperature has risen into the mid-forties, making it comfortable for sitting. Looking at the mountain peaks in the distance, I locate Mount Lyell at 13,114 feet, Mount Clark at 11,522, Cathedral Peak at 10,940, and Clouds Rest at 9,926. All are covered with a thick mantle of white, as are the granite features of the three canyons in front of me—Merced, Tenaya, and the main Yosemite. What I see was a long time in developing.

Four hundred fifty million years ago, the Sierra Nevada range that spreads out before me was a flat seabed off the Pacific coast which once ran through central Nevada off to my right. If the continent hadn't shifted, I'd be eating lunch under water instead of sitting almost two miles in the sky. As the earth's plates moved against each other, the ocean bottom folded into the air, creating these mountains and shifting the beach two hundred miles to the west. The Sierra continued to rise on its hinge, allowing the gently flowing waters of the newly formed Merced River and Tenaya Creek to pick up speed and carve the canyons three thousand feet deep. Then five million years ago the glaciers moved in and sharpened the top edges, widened and deepened the valley, and cut through hundreds of feet of solid bedrock. According to the generally accepted theory, the pile of rocks left by a retreating glacier from the last ice age, the terminal moraine, dammed the valley near El Capitan and created Lake Yosemite. Over the centuries, glacial droppings and sediments washed down from the sides of the mountains and filled in the lake, creating the valley meadows from mountain dust and glacial ice. These meadows have nourished a thousand generations of trees, birds, coyotes, and people, all evolving together.

While this geological history is easy to see from a mile above, it's hard to feel the truth of it. It seems too massive a project to have happened. Josiah Whitney, an early government authority on geology, stood here in the late 1800s and declared that the bottom of the mountains had simply dropped, creating this cathedral-like valley. Looking at the sheer verticality of the walls, I understand his conclusion; it's the simplest one. When John Muir looked, however, he saw complexity in the earth's formation and said, "No, 'twas glaciers." He then spent years measuring the scratches on mountain walls, comparing moraines, and locating the remnants of those ice flows. Muir's conclusion was right, and here it is, spread out below my feet in all its majesty, as I eat the last of my peanut butter and jelly sandwich.

Packing up the remains of lunch, and straightening the plastic bags in my shoes that are working surprisingly well, I look at the pine trees in the snow around me, then at the granite peaks within reach, and realize that something has changed. I no longer feel in a hurry. I sit back down and enjoy the peacefulness, the solitude of the breeze moving among the trees, for another hour. While listening to chickadees and nuthatches chirp and watching gray squirrels hop over the snow and dig for acorns, I realize that Yosemite is sharing its daily life with me. I'm outdoors and feel at home and would like to stay here in this ordinary moment when nothing special is happening. I want to continue breathing the cool mountain air, feeling the warm sun on my skin, and rubbing the boulder's rough granite with my hand because my heart physically feels part of the mountains.

But I can't. The sun has moved past high noon and is beginning its descent. Night will be coming. I have no food or shelter, and the day's accumulation of warmth is already beginning to seep away. Yet I'm grinning because I found something that I thought was lost: the closeness and awe I felt for nature when I was growing up. I cross Glacier Point with a bounce in my step and head for the Four Mile Trail that will take me back down into the valley. After six hours of arduous and slippery hiking, having met and conquered my challenge, the valley floor and something deliciously hot to drink are only an hour away. But on coming out from the woods and beginning the hike down the valley wall, I realize that the trail hasn't been seen since Glacier Point a mile back. I stop on a patch of snow, unable to tell if the trail continues straight ahead and goes around the bend or climbs up through the snow on my left. Maybe it made a turn somewhere in the woods behind me and I need to retrace my steps. Anxiety dumps the feelings of joy into the pit of my stomach as I shift gears and start making survival plans.

Going to the right is not an option because I'm on the edge of the canyon and there isn't anything but a great view and a mile drop into the valley. If I can walk forward fifty feet and make it around the bend, the trail might continue down out of the snow. Fifty feet is all that may be separating me from a quick hike down. Just a three-second dash! But there may not be a trail here. I may be standing on a snow bridge that is clinging to the side of the valley wall. How strong is the cohesive power of snow? I feel the snow shift underneath me and try not to move and shake an avalanche loose. But as I seriously consider going on, a chill snakes up my back. Only fifty feet! If I get over it and then the snow bridge falls and there's no trail to be found, how do I get back? To my left a snowbank with a slope of seventy degrees offers a second option. If I can climb up that and safely crawl over the corner of the precipice, I may be able to find the trail later on, if the trail goes that way, presuming I can safely come back down off the icy ridge. Slowly I back up, then try to scramble up the slope using my hands and feet, but the toes of my running shoes can kick only a couple inches into the hard snow and allow me to move up ten feet before I start sliding down toward the canyon's edge.

The sun is now halfway down in the sky and it will be getting dark in a few hours. There may not be enough time to make it back in daylight, and I don't know my way through these mountains. It's no longer a matter of whether a wild animal will happen to show up and do something violent or if a rockslide comes down on me. It's a matter of my needing to do something. It has to be the right decision, and the decision has to be made now. Or I am going to die.

"Enough!" I yell at my shoes, the snow, and the stupid trail. I decide that I don't want to die and that I can't safely make it down the last three miles because the trail is closed. "Fine time for that to sink in!" I mutter, along with other comments like "They did say the trail was closed." This means that I have to retrace the ten miles I just completed: thump back through the deep snow, slide across the icy trail from Illilouette, and hike down the chilled and slick steps of the Mist Trail . . . and do it in half the time. I head back at a jaunt.

Four hours later, as the last minutes of daylight fade and the cold of night settles in, I reach camp. My eyes are glazed over, my body is shaking, and I'm talking to a squirrel that I suspect is imaginary. But I'm also deliriously happy because I took a huge risk and survived. I heard an unfamiliar voice guide me through, and finally I feel connected to something bigger than my life.

Hiking Over the Edge

When we try to pick out anything by itself, we find it hitched
to everything else in the universe.

—John Muir, *My First Summer in the Sierra*

On this trip I intentionally aim to get lost. All the geological,
biological, and botanical facts about the valley, as well as all the
books I've read that were written by people who lived in Yosemite
over the centuries, are like dried raisins and salted nuts. They're
interesting to chew as trail food, but I can't use their experiences
to get close to nature. I have to use my own eyes and feet.

The wilderness is not the beautiful, inspiring scenery I once
thought it was. It's also not the heart of chaos that Joseph Con-
rad wrote about, where wild creatures are waiting behind trees
to spring out and kill me, although thoughts like this come to
mind when I'm hiking by myself and I can hear something large
go crashing through the forest. Nature is also not the Christ
revelation of God that others would have it be, as preachers
across the nation proclaimed in the early 1800s and German
artists like Caspar David Friedrich painted in the late 1800s, with
crucifixes and ethereal cathedrals appearing in the mountains

of their European landscapes as if nature had no personality or spirituality of its own.

Early Christian leaders like Justin Martyr and Athanasius had to deal with questions about nature from those who believed the Gnostic teachings about good and evil: the spirit is good, but the senses and all matter, including nature and apple pie, are evil. Justin and Athanasius believed that creation was good because it came from God, so it was proper to use our senses to enjoy its beauty. It was in Yosemite that John Muir found his Creator and in nature that Hildegard of Bingen saw her mystical revelations. I imagine that when Thomas Merton, a monk at Gethsemani Monastery, walked through the Kentucky woods during breaks from his theological studies, he remembered being a child and wandering the French countryside as his father painted landscapes. I think Merton felt drawn back to nature because it held answers about God's mystery that his books did not.

It's not that I want to see spirituality in the trees like the pantheists do, or decode messages left by Druidic elves in stones piled under gnarled oak trees on the talus behind Yosemite Village. But I do entertain this possibility with an impish fantasy. I want to appreciate the wonders of nature on the grand scale so evident here, and then watch the ordinary movements of nature back home in the city and see in them the sparks of creation that continue to flame, thrust, and find expression in everything that lives. I want the experience of the Native Americans who regarded the coyote and bear as kin, who heard wisdom in the running streams, and who felt the presence and spirit of each part of creation. I want to reclaim the sense of enchantment I used to feel as a child when I played in the woods and touch the primordial powers spoken about in the myths that guided primitive cultures. I seek the mystery beneath the surface of the

unkempt wilderness because I need to know that the chaos of my
life is rooted in something solid underneath. I want to experience
the whole of life, the holy now, with all of its tasty side dishes.

⤳

In March the transition from winter to spring begins as unrelent-
ing cold yields to a few hours of warmth in the middle of each
day. Patches of green push through clumps of brown grass as
the meadows thaw into islands of mush. The songs of blackbirds
find welcomed responses in other creatures returning to their
spring homes, and trails that wind their way up the steep valley
walls begin to clear of ice and snow. After the tent is set up in
Camp 4, I walk around the valley delighting in the fresh, clean
air and adjusting to the presence of mountains looming a mile
above me at every turn. Then smaller sights magically appear, like
200-foot-tall Sugar pines that were somehow invisible before. I
notice an American dipper playing in the rapids, hear the creeks
trickling, and smell the aroma of pine needles. When I sit down
on a log and take a deep breath, the rush of four hours of driving to get here falls off. Then I notice a bird, hidden in the trees
twenty feet away, cleaning the sides of its beak on a branch and
a coyote watching me intently from the shadows of a bush, and
I believe everything about this place once again.

   Although the days are getting milder, reaching the mid-fifties
and making rock climbing less of an endurance contest with the
weather, the unsettledness of the air, caught in the tussle between
the warm days and cold nights, creates dynamic displays of clouds
that stretch to the stratosphere. Sunrise is often a grand show as
miles of clouds, spread across the breadth of the sky, shift from
orange to red to pink. The entire event is over in ten minutes

and everyone who is asleep has no clue that a gaudy light show has just flashed across the sky. This morning there are no bright colors. Gray clouds are stacked on top of each other and darkness is filtering down through the layers like espresso poured slowly into steamed milk. Throughout the morning, scattered showers skip over the valley like adolescents with hoses. By noon most of the low storm clouds that threatened everyone's plans have moved on, leaving the higher billowy cumulus. I hike the trail to the top of Yosemite Falls and watch clouds on the Sierra crest being rolled into long bales like hay as the wind sweeps up the curved flanks of the mountains.

Late in the afternoon, charcoal black clouds descend to the top of the canyon walls, blocking the sun and making the valley nearly as dark as night, as if a medieval eclipse has been set in motion with wooden gears and levers clacking into grooves, chocks tumbling, and crude iron-shod wheels rumbling over the mountains. Brooding clouds like these in the Midwest generally mean that severe thunderstorms are about to let loose with everything in their bag of tricks. I'm on a wooded talus several hundred feet above the horse stables with a grand view of the drama developing over the length of the valley, and I'm torn between heading for safety or lingering to see if anything exciting develops. I often did this in Wisconsin, too, when tornado sirens sounded. Then, instead of running down into the basement, I'd hurry outside to an open space and watch the tornado approach.

A shaft of light breaks through the blackness and shoots an intense band of light on the valley wall between Middle Brother and Columbia Rock. There's no light anywhere else in the valley, just the shimmering bar of gold. The band is so intense that its reflection creates shadows on the wrong side of trees. The glow lasts fifteen minutes, starts to fade, and is gone, leaving the valley pitch black again. I make my way carefully down the dark trail, trying not to step over the side edge.

Then light explodes through a hole in the black clouds beyond El Capitan, down by Bridalveil Fall, making the entire west end of the valley glow reddish-gold. It reminds me of Albert Bierstadt's painting *Sunset in the Yosemite Valley,* which has extremely dark tones and a glorious light glowing in one corner. I pooh-poohed the work as an example of Bierstadt taking artistic license. Not anymore. The light hits the surface of the Merced River and sends a line of orange fire streaking up the water toward me. I hurry into the meadow to get a clearer view without trees in the way, then run toward the west drawn by this Bierstadt incarnation of heaven on earth. Two birds dart across the path, fleeing something unseen to the right. By the time I reach Sentinel Meadow the glow has doubled. In the middle of Swinging Bridge I stop, heart pounding, so near a Presence that I do not want to get any closer. All of nature seems hushed in awe and the cryptic words come: "Only the splendor of Light hides Thee!" The glowing floods the valley like a four-thousand-foot tsunami, engulfing the valley in luminescence.

When the flood of light ebbs after five minutes and pulls back into the western end of the valley, the tranquil blue, purple, and rose colors of evening seep back into the meadow from the dark sides of the valley where they were pushed by the wall of light. Birds return to their trees and chirp in relief; night begins its appointed rounds. But I am still breathless, disoriented, mute.

In his journal, John Muir often wrote about seeing similar wonders, using effusive words to describe the glories around him: "I am feasting in the Lord's mountain house, and what pen may write my blessings!" Such praise wasn't unusual in his day, as everyone spoke in religious terms then. When he describes an experience by stringing scripture to scripture, he was in the throes of something he couldn't describe in common words. He was searching for a higher language and Christian references were the highest he knew.

What excites me about Muir's study of nature are not the grand discoveries but the limitations, and my belief, in a T. S. Eliot kind of awareness, that the end of any scientific study will always circle us back to where we started: amazed at the infinite complexity of nature and appreciating its beauty even more. We can pick apart the elements that make up a natural scene as much as we want, organizing what looks to be chaos into levels of relative understanding, the genus and phylum, then, moving smaller in our observations, past the mitochondria and ribosomes, until we get below the size of atoms into the subatomic particles, the muons and quarks ... and realize that we're swimming in mystery again and don't know what in the world is going on. Scientists are moved by the wonder they discover in their work, and often their scientific descriptions come out sounding like mystical experiences.

Humans have a drive to understand the origins of everything. We mentally push the land masses of earth back together like clumps of clay, trying to piece together how they were once joined. We pick the planet up in our fingers like a marble, place it in relation to the immensity of the Milky Way, then zoom away and see just how invisible we are to the rest of the universe. We can collapse all our Big Bang theories into the pinprick of the universe's origin, rushing backward to the beginning of time and waxing as eloquently as we want about our beginnings. Yet our best scientific conclusions, as well as our most astute theological statements, are apt to be wild guesses because there is too much we don't understand about the mythology of physics or the quantum mechanics of God.

Advances in technology haven't helped. Scientists recently concluded that there must be a great deal of dark matter in the universe, ancient stars that burned out which are invisible to us, and that the gravitational mass of these invisible white dwarfs is what holds the spiral galaxies together. At the same time, this dark matter is also what pulls the universe apart. Scientists are like mountain climbers: both groups live on the edges of society, both seek the chaotic, passionate spirit of Creation, and both aren't afraid to poke their fingers into the unknown to see what's there.

The next afternoon I drive up to Glacier Point a mile above the valley floor to watch the sunset. I stand on the edge of the valley wall facing Half Dome to the east and watch the last daylight leave the Sierra Nevada range and color the mountain peaks crimson red. As darkness fills the valley and rises up toward me, I get lost in the broader sweep of the land and feel the power that swelled up from below to form these granite mountains. The alpenglow continues to fade from rose to purple to blue, and the features of earth lessen until they can no longer be seen. Standing in the darkness of the sky on the top of the mountain, I count the stars down from the North Star as they appear, until stars twinkle all around me, even down to the level of my knees. I can no longer see my feet or remember how close I'm standing to the edge of the canyon. I think I'm a solid foot away.

Here between the civilization of the constellations of campfires in the valley below and the eternity of the fires of stars burning above, exists the wilderness of black bear and mountain lion, of coyote and hawk. A few other people who are close by are also mesmerized by this glory. What I thought was a solitary search for mystery also pulls on the hearts of others.

Drawing Close to Sacred Land

Climb the mountains and get their good tidings. Nature's
peace will flow into you as sunshine flows into trees.

—John Muir, *Our National Parks*

With April's warmer weather, rock climbers return like birds to
their nesting places on the valley walls, filling campsites around
me. We casually chat as they prepare for their adventures. I nod
and pretend to understand, but in my tent at night I read about
their daring craft, wondering if I will ever have the nerve to climb.

No matter what part of the world they're from, the Camp 4
community interacts with each other like old acquaintances,
even if they've just met, because they share a common language
and goal. People stop by to find out where everyone is climbing tomorrow. The camp bulletin board is covered with notices
from people looking for climbing partners or with gear to sell,
scribbled on whatever was available—notebook paper, the inside
of cereal boxes, even toilet paper, a precious commodity when
camping, but hard to read because the ink bleeds:

Partner wanted. I can lead 5.10 route. Not looking for the foolhardy. In the valley for one week, but floating from campsite to campsite. Antwon.

Lost a Scarpa approach shoe at the Nutcracker. Fell into the bushes to the right. If found, please contact John in 23.

Mike. Chamo, gi estas en la area, deja saber donde estas?

Anyone going to Vancouver around the 6th? I need a ride. Will share gas. George (Or to Washington state. Or Portland. Even the 7th or 8th works.)

Carol, we're climbing Cookie Cliff. Meet you there.

Belgian climber looking for a partner. See Francois, site 21.

I don't know most of the 140 climbers here. Every morning after breakfast I head out and hike for most of the day and stop in briefly for dinner before going for a short walk in the evening. When I come back to camp, I sleep. What talking I do is primarily with the people who are camping in my site but only when we happen to be eating at the same time. Most of our longer sharing happens on days that are either rainy or after an all-day hike when my legs need to rest.

Around camp people say things like "climbing is his religion" and "the soul of the mountain." Over breakfast I ask Ted what this is about. He's in the red tent next to my yellow one. He says there's an underlying sense of spirituality to climbing, but it generally isn't talked about. It's a presence that climbers feel more than a statement of faith. Spirituality is developing a close relationship with something, and for Ted this means sharing an experience with a natural object, whether it's a fifteen-foot boulder or a mile-high valley wall. Not to conquer it by getting on top, but working with it as he learns to read its bumps and cracks, feeling its strength and personality in his hands. Frank says, as he struggles to crawl out of his tiny bivy tent and pull on his boots and insulated vest for the mid-forty-degree air, that he just loves the rush of energy he gets from a really radical climb where he takes a lot of risks and doesn't break any bones. I think Frank has been here for a couple of weeks, moving from site to site to keep ahead of the rangers checking camping permits.

Rachael shuffles over from the site next door in her hooded Berkeley sweater. She clears space for her steaming cup of coffee on our weathered picnic table that has been tattooed with the cooking burns and carved with the initials of several generations of climbers. I think she and Ted are checking each other out because she is often hanging around our campsite. She views climbing as a holistic challenge, a discipline she prepares for throughout the year by working out. "It's a test not just of my physical abilities but also of my mental strength and courage. Out of this challenge comes insight into who I am and, if I'm lucky, a glimpse into the nature of the Luminous Entity." Surprised by the creative possibilities of her image, I ask what she means. She says, "Just wait. You'll see it sometime this week."

Ted's partner, Scott, who arrived yesterday after climbing at Joshua Tree in Southern California, says climbers are more concerned about the ethics of climbing, which rise out of their respect for the mountain. "Technological innovations," he says, "have made a number of options possible, but not all of them are good. Now, instead of taking an hour to drill a hole, hammer a metal spike in, move up ten feet, and do it again, people can punch bolts into the rock with power tools, from the bottom of a climb to the top, and essentially walk up a long ladder. But pure climbing runs counter to sport climbing, where the only goal is to finish as fast as possible. Pure climbing is getting to

...e top using as few removable aids as you can, and sharing the experience with your partners. It's honoring the mountain." I read that in the 1950s climbing pioneer Royal Robbins was upset with Warren Harding for pounding metal objects like stove legs into cracks for safety wherever he wanted one and defacing the rock, rather than finding a natural route.

Frank thinks it's pretty cool that our tents are on the site of an Ahwahnechee camp and that when we show reverence for nature, we pick up some of their spirituality.

Walking by with a towel on his way to the bathroom, Tom hears a serious discussion going on and makes a detour. He loves philosophical debates and loves to talk, but I haven't seen him go out on any climbs and I'm beginning to wonder if he just talks to people around camp all day. He says that Yosemite is the premier training ground for world-class climbers even though difficult climbs are being explored all around the world for several reasons. First, Yosemite has the best concentration of the three climbing disciplines: big wall, free climbing, and bouldering. Second, when he's climbing in the valley, there's a feeling he can't describe but it keeps drawing him back. He looks at me, somehow figures I'm not a climber, and asks what I'm doing here. "Following John Muir's footsteps," I say. "The first time Muir saw Yosemite, he found something greater than himself. He was in awe of the stunning beauty of the valley and hiking through these mountains he discovered his passion for life."

Tom says, "I admire Muir for free climbing mountain peaks without equipment. Tough dude. Are you as tough?"

"When I need to be."

But he gives me a look that says I will have to prove this to him.

Tom goes back to the conversation and says that speed climbing the big walls can be good or bad, depending on whether the climber takes time to enjoy the route or regards the mountain as the enemy, something to fight against. "Climbing fast and without protection in case you fall is dangerous but it puts you in the arena with the big boys: trusting the mountain with your life. But if you're doing it just to beat someone else's time, then forget it. It's not worth anything. To anybody."

Climbing in Yosemite was a sporadic activity until the middle part of the twentieth century, when innovators like Harding, Robbins, and Yvon Chouinard made their own equipment in blacksmith shops to deal with the hardness of the granite as well as the height and sheer verticality of the walls. Their creations made climbing significantly safer, although climbers still die every year. In the 1960s climbing became popular as more people dropped out of society and headed back to nature. My friend John Westlake was one of them who climbed walls all around the valley, including El Capitan and Half Dome. He has told me stories about the climbers in camp who became famous, stories that never made the newspapers. His battered hands still bear witness to his dedication. Climbers today are generally in their twenties and thirties, with a few younger and a scattering older, of average height but no paunch. They have strong upper bodies and legs, great abs, and banged-up knuckles and knees. Clothing is often colorful, as are the colors of the tents that make the camp look like a small village. Leggings, felt vests, well-worn shoes, and an eclectic variety of stocking caps complete the picture. Each year more females climb and now make up 20 percent of the total.

Rock climbers have a gung-ho attitude and a look in their eyes, unburdened by guilt or doubt, that says, "We can conquer anything!" If they can't get up a route, they will strategize with others, physically train, and try until they succeed. Climbing teaches humility, perseverance, and teamwork. Ripped tendons and broken bones are part of the adventure. Losing your grip, falling off the side of a mountain, and having your rope jerk you back to safety ten or twenty feet down is such a common occurrence that few give it a second thought.

Days between climbs are spent recuperating in hammocks, preparing equipment, researching routes, gathering one's mental resources, and finding partners. Some climbers like Frank party hard after a climb. Some are vegetarian. Some are too tightly wound and have a list of climbs that they are going to do no matter what the weather. Some have the fatalism common to their generation, not caring if they survive their twenties. Some are philosophers of stone like Tom, who will talk to you late into the night about the mythology and theology of mountains until you find an excuse to slip away. By 10:00 p.m. the camp quiets down out of respect for those who will climb, and risk their lives, tomorrow. When climbers return after a multi-day excursion, there are hearty congratulations. Tired smiles show that they know they have accomplished something significant, not just the completion of a difficult route but also the conquering of a personal challenge.

Climbers are aware that if they make a mistake, they can be seriously injured, even die. Yet they push themselves to the edge of their abilities and to the limits of their equipment, so that they will experience a different world and discover strengths hidden within them. There's a chance that they will not measure up to the demands of a climb and fail, and they accept this as part of the challenge. If they can't fail, if there's not a chance that they can get hurt, then to them the challenge isn't real. They want to know what human existence has to offer, and they will push against every limit in order to reach the boundary, then tightrope along this frail edge, hoping they don't lean the wrong way.

A few will keep climbing as they break more and more bones, and attempt increasingly risky and dangerous routes until their final fall. And they are at peace with this.

Don and Susan, in their mid-thirties, arrived yesterday in Rachael's site, and say they are searching for more than a steady job that will get them to retirement. They want to see life without filters. They want to slam themselves against the rock and be surrounded by the power of the mountains, hole up on a ledge during a thunderstorm and feel the breath of the Great Spirit in the clouds swirling around them, learn how to keep their fears in check while climbing over stone that is disintegrating in their hands, and discover just how much they love life. And they want to know if they can trust each other to be strong when lives are on the line.

The most dangerous part of climbing is in the area where you have already pushed yourself to the breaking point and are one handhold from either falling or being able to go on. The challenge is to know when to pull back, climb down for half an hour, and start up a different route versus when to continue on, let go of your last safe hold, hug the flat rock, and trust the moist friction of your skin to stick to the slick granite surface long enough to reach a blind hold that now has to be there—all while three thousand feet above the ground. These are the moments when you learn the truth about yourself. Sometimes you try a move that others have tried and it works, like the pendulum swing that allows climbers to jump to the other side of a blank section of wall. Sometimes the moves don't work. Yesterday Frank tried a layback on an iffy piece of stone. It gave way and he fell ten feet and then bounced sideways off a rock, but his rope held. He climbed back up, tried again, and made it. Today he's happy, but really sore.

Most of the time Camp 4 looks like an open-air dorm. Laundry hangs on tent lines and sleeping bags wet from a recent storm are draped over branches. People line up for access to the bathroom and the one sink where we can clean cooking pots in a way that won't attract bears. Climbers generally don't care how they look, and cleanliness is based on functional needs. Being stuck on a rock without a shower after days of continual exercise reduces one's sensitivity to smells.

As one group returns to camp after a climb and unloads their gear, including the hanging platform they slept on (basically a nylon cot without legs tethered to a single peg in the wall), I hear them say, "Well, that was the poorest design of a portaledge I've ever seen!" "Yeah, you really get to know your partner's feet. I thought my feet smelled bad!" "O man, a blister on my foot! When did that happen?"

Louisa and her group from Spain are sleeping in today, not having slept much on El Capitan during their five-day climb. She's up first and spends hours sitting by the fire, staring into the flames. The rest of her group will get up in the afternoon. Wandering over, I ask what she's been thinking about for so long. Louisa says, "I'm going over the climb and remembering the joy, the beauty of being part of the mountain and seeing what it sees, even if just for a few days. Also the moments of terror when you lose your nerve, unsure what to do next. Then you get your focus back and the fear passes. As long as you stay focused on the technical aspects, the fear stays gone, the beauty of the climb takes over, and your movements flow again with the rock. You move together and dance with the mountain. Sometimes the line is very thin between daring and danger, but we're not machines, you know, doing the route exactly as others have done it. I need to express my creativity, my joy. Not too much, just enough to make the climb my own."

I mention that Muir once froze while climbing across the face of Mount Ritter, unsure what to do next but knowing that if he didn't move soon, his muscles would tire, he'd fall, and he'd most likely die. "What did he do?" Louisa asks. "He stayed put until the fear passed, confidence returned, and he finished the climb." Shaking her head, she says, "If you can't get rid of the fear, if you worry that every move you make might be the wrong one, you will be timid and you will make mistakes. Then you need to get down because you are a danger to your partners."

Climbers find their answers in life by climbing. Every day they head out to see what they can stir up, what challenges can be overcome, and what connections they can make with nature, all in the hope that they will return to camp in one piece. I can't remember the last time I went through a day worried that I might die. It's a frequent thought here, and it keeps me energized and focused.

The risks that climbers take each day encourage me to push my own adventures closer to the edge of where prudent ends and foolhardy begins. I plunge into overgrown trails to see where they go: trails that were abandoned because they were no longer safe due to rock slides, poisonous snakes, or animals with large teeth that like to jump on humans sauntering alone through the forest. I like to see how far into the mountains I can hike and still get back before dark. I get a thrill scrambling up crumbly mountaintops, keeping my balance on the shifting surfaces, and gazing over the grand vistas because doing this makes me feel alive. While my adventures don't need to be life-threatening, they do have to be physically demanding and involve some risk. Hiking by myself in the wilderness puts me in this situation, as much as Evelyn always wished that I would stop doing it.

As I return to camp at dusk after a day exploring the east end of the valley and the huge medial moraine between Happy Isles and Mirror Lake, three climbers, each about six-foot-five, head the other way, out for some nighttime adventure. They're dressed completely in black with coils of rope over their shoulders. With single-beam climbing lights in the middle of their foreheads, they look like Hesiod's three Cyclops brothers out to secretly test new equipment they made in their blacksmith shop.

Before dawn, I hike up the trail on the canyon wall to the overlook at Columbia Point, one thousand feet above the valley floor, waiting for the sunrise over the mountains. I lower my expectations for how glorious this dawn will be, wanting to regard whatever happens as a grace. To borrow a Japanese Buddhist image, I must empty my begging bowl in order to receive not what I think I need but what is being offered, and to regard whatever comes as *oryoki*—just enough. I'm bundled against the morning's cold and the sharp bite of the moisture-ladened air feels refreshing on my face. Waiting for the sun to rise above the horizon is no longer a matter of faith as it was for my ancestors. I know the sun will show up on its own. No bonfires have to be lit to encourage it to return from the depths of the cosmos.

Darkness holds both illumination and illusion. Which one do I seek? I'm not looking for a unified theology in nature that will answer every question. No, I am looking for the mystery of life, even if it can't be solved but only hiked further into. Darkness, as well as the despair, anger, and emptiness I've felt since Ev's death, live inside me; I try to fill the space with endless activities. There are also the common feelings of displeasure, selfishness, and jealousy that I keep hidden and unresolved, even knowing that I will not grow as a person until my own wilderness is faced.

This morning I set my doubts aside and celebrate spring's resurrection from dead winter. Like Muir, I will worship more deeply in the open air this Easter than if I were enclosed in a church building and unable to see the mountains. I don't need fine clothes, brass choirs, or huge displays of flowers. The birds will be my choir. I'm wearing clothes that keep me warm; flowers like crimson columbine, monkey flower, and mountain lupine are blooming around me.

Seeing light break the horizon before I do, the birds around me begin singing. The suddenness of their loud chirping clangs against the silence of the last ten hours like Buddhist cymbals scaring away the demons of the night. The birds sing with gratefulness for a new day of life, as they do every morning, not saving their praises for the high holy days but singing happily for this moment that holds the sacred and giving themselves to it. As the sun rises over the far horizon with the orange fire of dawn, dots of brilliance flash off the tops of the bare granite peaks and domes of the Sierra Nevada. The highlands above me are lit while the valley below continues to wait in darkness. When the sun reaches the nook of Illilouette Canyon, it sends a focused beam through the narrow gap between the mountains and illuminates Cook's Meadow in warm, yellow light, while Leidig and Sentinel Meadows wait patiently in the dark. I hike back down into the valley, humming and celebrating the Great Spirit of the world, who has the wisdom to share the joy of life with animals, flowers, and birds.

In the highlands, snow is melting over the roots of a hundred thousand trees. The upland watershed collects this water and sends it tumbling down steep canyons and rumbling over falls as the rivers renew their voices. Every year some flooding occurs in the valley as the snow melts and overruns a few of the campsites, usually those at the east end of the valley. I don't know how extensive the flooding is predicted to be this year, but the snow pack is fairly thick and this morning the trail that I used last night to pass through Leidig Meadow is barely visible above the spreading water. The snow cone at the bottom of Yosemite Falls is melting and frazil ice is flowing like white slurry through its delta.

On a whim I decide to see how fast I can hike from Happy Isles to Nevada Fall, setting aside my hard-fought decision to slow down and see the details of nature for the sheer thrill of a physical challenge. I head off with a burst of energy and reach the top of Vernal Fall in thirty-five minutes. Feeling proud, I don't even pause to catch my breath or marvel that the river is overflowing the viewing area at the top of Vernal. Instead I push on past the gray color of Emerald Pool, hoping to set a new personal record. Five minutes later I have to stop. Water roaring down the canyon has washed away the bridge over the river that leads to Nevada Fall. I presumed it would have survived because it was made of steel not wood, but it's missing, broken off its concrete moorings by the force of the water hurtling through the river channel and washed downstream to where the river stores the trinkets it collects during storms.

FLOODS AND ROCKSLIDES

The springtime melting of snow in the high country typically results in the valley's rivers overflowing. Cabins have been built out of the annual flood zones, but every twenty years an overabundance of snow, or a combination of weather

factors, results in greater flooding and damage to some of
the permanent buildings. The 1955 flood covered two-thirds
of the valley floor. Approximately every one hundred years
a sustained, heavy rain melts the snow so quickly that the
entire valley floods, eroding roads, destroying water and
sewer systems, and carrying cabins away.

Falling boulders and small rockslides are also common oc-
currences in Yosemite Valley. The talus piles at the bottom
of the cliffs bear witness to this. Rocks often break loose
over winter, leaving white spots on the walls, especially in
the area between Glacier Point and Sentinel Rock. Because
of the hardness of the granite and the wide spacing of the
joints, massive rockslides are infrequent and people are
seldom hurt. The area just west of El Capitan known as
the Rockslides is a notable exception.

After coming back down the Mist Trail, I walk along the dry
southern edge of the valley floor, following the trail that goes
behind the LeConte Memorial and over to the chapel, crossing
the river on the Swinging Bridge. During the two hours I spent
higher in the mountains, the flood has expanded and buried the
trail under two feet of water. My choice is to either walk around
the meadow in forty minutes or go through one hundred feet
of near-freezing water in two. Hot from the hike, I choose the
wet route, rolling my pants above my knees and taking off my
shoes. Halfway across, in cold water that was snow only hours
ago, pain shoots through my legs before they go numb. When I
reach dry land, I flop down and rub my legs, grimacing as warm
blood flows back in.

　What did Native Americans do when the valley flooded?

It's not like they could shove all their belongings into a car and quickly drive away. How did they cope with being at the mercy of natural forces strong enough to wipe out the entire tribe with one flash flood roaring down the canyon, or one unending blizzard freezing and burying the valley, or the massive influx of starving mountain lions and bears? They lived without the benefit of hourly newscasts yet knew how to read the wind, the clouds, and the changes in temperature.

As the pain subsides, I have an overwhelming desire to hike up the steep switchbacks to Columbia Point again to see what all this water looks like from above. An hour later I reach the overlook by the rock with a metal U.S. Geological seal, hot again from the hike up and now wishing for cold water to cool down. Leaning on the metal railing, I gaze over the wide expanse of the pool-laden meadows. This is what land on earth once looked like, with rivers and creeks flowing close to each other and flowers blooming everywhere, in the time before cities, farms, and factories consolidated streams into concrete channels, drained marshes, and leveled the wooded hills. The abundance of Eden is spread out before me—moist, fertile, and filled with thousands of interacting life forms.

John Muir looked over the valley many times, and I'd like to think that he felt the same way I do. In his journals he describes how the course of the Merced River went from side to side through the valley as it flowed from Happy Isles in the east to El Portal in the west, nudged to the left by the outwash from Indian Canyon then to the right by the glacial moraine at the foot of Sentinel Rock, and back and forth again as it flowed down the valley, influenced by other moraines, tributaries, and rockslides. His words are on display in front of me. He also said that a rockfall had covered most of the glacial moraine near Sentinel Rock, and trees blocked his observations. I stare at that area but can only perceive a slight rise in the land. Marshy areas were drained since Muir's time and more trees have grown up and filled in the valley, changing the landscape of what he saw 140 years ago. Yet the geologic forces he identified are still influencing the course of the Merced River.

Seamus Heaney of Ireland says that the landscape of one's home is always sacramental. It's part of our blood. The land we live on changes and shapes us. It molds our character and it's the soil out of which we grow. It's where we either encounter the divine or we never make the connection. Drawing on his years as a farmer in Kentucky, Wendell Berry says that we need to enter into a sacred partnership with the land, growing crops on it to feed ourselves while taking care to minimize the harm we do to it and to the animals and birds living there. We can sustain each other, like this valley and the Ahwahnechees did. Reverence for the land is where our understanding of ourselves begins.

After a dinner of stew and peas, I wander through Leidig Meadow and watch a dozen robins chase each other, soaring and swooping low over the ground like miniature fighter pilots. I sit in an open place by the river as the light of day and the dark of night begin to exchange places. When the sun begins its final setting, the clouds around the quarter moon are pale yellow. On a whim, I dare Evelyn—if she is still around and watching over me from her new celestial home—to do something with the clouds. In that moment a rich yellow glow spreads across the entire sky.

Can this be a coincidence? I feel a bit spooked, but for the first time I sense that Evelyn is telling me she is okay where she is and I don't have to worry about her anymore. The glow lasts ten minutes. When it begins to fade, I feel her saying good-bye and taking her place among the stars as they process across the dark heavens in their great fellowship. "Thank you, my love," I say, and the cosmic night settles around me.

West End Trails

Before dawn I head toward the west end as watercolor shades of pink and yellow suffuse the valley. The air is cool, perfect for a hike through the meadows. When I reach El Capitan an hour later the sun is beginning to rise over the horizon. I scramble up the talus slope to watch Fred, Jeff, and Jordan climb. I met them last night while waiting in line to use the pay phones by the parking lot. With only three phones for all the campers, the wait can be long. It will be interesting to see if they can work together, balancing Jordan's drive and their safety concerns. Yesterday Jeff said that Jordan was a bold climber who just goes, often free climbing the first ten pitches while the rest of them are carefully placing safety gear in the rock. Jordan thought I was a climber, saying that I had the build, and he should know. Last night he always knew a little bit more than whatever I had to say.

The guys are on the Wall of the Early Morning Light, which earned its name because El Cap protrudes into the valley and this part catches the first rays of dawn. Jordan is leading, now about eighty feet up, and looking for small cracks he can either wedge a piton into or jam and hook with his fingers. Jeff has just stepped off the ground and is five feet up. I tug on his pants and he grins with excitement. Fred is sitting on the ground looking bored as he keeps the lines clear until his time comes. For seven days they will test themselves, and their friendship, on the rock. When my neck gets tired of looking up, I head off, skirting the discarded empty cans strewn below—sliced fruit, chili, spaghetti, beer, and little brown bags with fecal aromas.

The west end of the valley is generally ignored because all the campsites and places for people are in the east. I wander around in leisure, spontaneously following trails as they appear, not knowing where I'll end up. I don't know these woods. By the river on the far side of one meadow I find a metal plaque bolted to a large boulder that commemorates where the Mariposa Battalion spent its first night in the valley in 1851. I get a thrill thinking of Lafayette Bunnell sitting here with the first non-Natives to enter the valley, struggling to find words capable of describing the majesty of El Capitan rising up in front of him. Eventually he would write, "I have seen the power and glory of a Supreme Being."

On the other side of the meadow, by the road that leads to Bridalveil Fall, a historical marker reports that John Muir camped here with Teddy Roosevelt. The story is that Muir snuck the president away from his official group ensconced in the heated cabins at the Wawona grove of giant sequoias, and the two of them camped at Glacier Point. Overnight two feet of snow fell and as they dug themselves out, Roosevelt said something like, "Bully good!" Muir persuaded him to save the rest of Yosemite. Then they came down into the valley and camped on this spot. When Ralph Waldo Emerson visited Yosemite, Muir also tried to lure him away to sleep on the ground, but the old Transcendentalist liked to keep his distance, preferring to think about nature rather than hike in it. Perhaps he was feeling his age.

Upriver I find a place away from the history markers so that I will be free to think about the valley instead of thinking about them, eventually settling on a sandy beach with an unobstructed view of El Capitan. Through binoculars I watch climbers on narrow ledges thousands of feet above the valley floor prepare for today's climb. Some are eating breakfast and waiting on their portaledges for the sun to edge around to the west side of El Cap's nose and warm them from the night's cold so they can bend their fingers and begin climbing. Fred, Jeff, and Jordan are now about two hundred feet above tree level.

A great deal of Merced River water is surging past my view, although just how much is hard to gauge by how effortlessly and calmly it slides by. Rocks on the pebbled river bottom show through the deep water's amber color, pushing up gently on the underside of the water's surface to dimple it from below while overhanging trees dapple it from above with sunlight and shadows. Kinglets and warblers skim low over the river. Steller's jays fly down to a small pool and drink. A Brewer's blackbird lands to check me out, peering with its small yellow eyes that I don't find endearing, trying to encourage me to toss it food I don't have. Across the river a coyote trots into an opening and lets me see him for a moment, then turns and disappears into the woods. My friend Molly thinks that Coyote is my spirit guide. Considering how often a coyote seems to show up at significant moments, I'm beginning to think she's right.

A honeybee finds something of interest in the granite sand at my feet and spends minutes checking it out in detail. An intent little armored beetle crawls by, completely unmindful of my presence; I'm simply the source of a shadow that is cooling the sand. It has no idea that world-famous El Capitan is across the river. In relation to the insect, I'm as big as that. If the insect wanted to climb me the task might take an hour, if it laid out its route just right and was in a hurry. Afterward it could tell stories to its offspring about the time it climbed the warm mountain. Myths would develop, maybe an entire pantheon of gods based upon the lint it found in my pockets. The particles of breakfast ambrosia caught in the crevices of my clothing might be the inspiration for little beetle ballads! Maybe not.

Upriver a small rapids sparkles in the still-young light of the day, as do the fan-like leaves on dozens of quaking aspens lining the bank. The cool breeze coming along the course of the river balances the growing warmth of the day, and I set aside the bundle of thoughts and feelings that I carry with me and listen. I hear small birds chirping, the river flowing, and waterfalls cascading in the distance, their voices gaining strength as the rising sun melts more snow in the highlands and sends the water their way. The smells on the breeze are of a not-yet-formed day—hints of various meadow plants, marshy areas slowly drying, and something else. Rain? Perhaps. Because of the height of the canyon walls I can't see if storm clouds are approaching on the horizon, but there is a gray tint to the sky that wasn't there earlier.

Around noon it begins to rain and I head into the woods to listen to the sounds of the forest in a storm. Along the river, by the Housekeeping Camp, a dozen trees have already been undercut by this year's flood and fallen into the water. Others are leaning. One tree was brutally torn away, leaving its bank-side roots attached to the ground. In the area in front of the LeConte Memorial the land sharply drops thirty feet because of the erosive work of past floods. Over in the woods beneath the cliffs the mountain peaks dissolve and disappear in the low clouds and the valley floor visually becomes the highest point of land. Nothing can be seen above the trees except white sky. When the clouds shift, parts of the valley wall reappear like hovering phantoms. But without the rest of the mountain I no longer recognize what I'm looking at. Mist slips behind outcroppings on the wall and highlights them like statues lining a great hall.

Standing motionless with the trees, I listen to the rain showering through the branches, dripping on leaves and running over ground that is already soaked. With each rumble of thunder the ducks talk excitedly on the swollen river that is giving them more places where they can paddle. Granules of yellow pine pollen fall onto a pool in the path and draw together in geometric patterns. My thoughts join the pollen's swirling movement as granules break apart and reform in new configurations. Standing motionless, immersed in the sounds of the woods in the rain, I lose my awareness of being separate from the trees. We stand together, listening to the sounds of rain falling into the wilderness.

After an hour of not moving the chill penetrates my clothes. I leave to get something hot to drink at Degnan's store. Falling rain patters on the roof over the patio. Soaked by the storm, more Brewer's blackbirds show up looking for food, shaking water off and trying to look presentable. One swells up in size to chase off a competitor, but the challenger feints and comes around the other side of the table. They both look so miserable that I'd like to take a towel and dry them off.

Gary Snyder, a poet who once built trails in Yosemite and now lives in the foothills of the Sierra Nevada, incorporates Buddhist and Native American concepts into his writings about the spirit of nature. I haven't thought much about Buddhism and nature, but it makes as much sense as connecting Christianity with the outdoors. Christianity emphasizes using the natural resources of the world for the benefit of humans. Buddhism says that all life is holy and we should seek to live in harmony with nature instead of using it up. Yet, in spite of their different theologies, Christian and Buddhist societies have both abused nature in significant ways. Native Americans did a far better job of respecting the earth, protecting its sacredness and learning about the different spirits of its creatures. In Christianity the Celts of the fifth and sixth centuries, with their creative mix of Christian and Druid elements, were probably the most responsible, living in a personal relationship with the land.

➷

After a dry night, a small but intense storm moves into the valley with heavy showers for most of the day. Late in the afternoon the rain ends and the sun returns. I go into Leidig Meadow for the last hour of light with no plans other than to enjoy the scents and colors of an evening in the mountains. Birds chat away and frogs join in with their throaty chorus. People wander out to watch the lingering cumulus clouds in the west as they catch dusk's tangerine light and carry the glowing sunset tens of thousands of feet into the sky, making the valley's mile-high walls seem short, as if they were the two-foot banks of the river we're rafting down.

Ted and Rachael walk out from the climbers' camp and watch the sky deepen to a rich burnished gold color that makes the newly washed mountains shine with grandeur. The flooding has receded a bit, and with the sky reflecting off the water to the sides of the trail, people going through Leidig Meadow appear to be walking across water. Quietly talking among ourselves, Rachael leans over to me and says, "This is what I meant by the Luminous Entity, a glorious, natural scene that takes your breath away and speaks of deeper things." We marvel over the unexpected gift of this bright, colorful sunset before it dissolves and night's darkness closes in.

I watch as one person is drawn away from the path into the soaked meadow. He lifts his hat off, turns around as he takes in the glory of the mountains glowing around him, and walks into the tall grass, enticed, then overcome by the light, until he goes down into a lower section of land and is seen no more. After a time he emerges on the other side of the ocean of grass, reaches out and touches a 180-foot ponderosa pine that dwarfs him. They stand together in silhouette, watching the sunset. After

a while he puts his hand down and continues walking into the
next meadow, further into something he's found, further into his
place of mind, further into the shadows of evening where he is
lost to my view, lost to time that marks the passage of journeys
in this world and to the mysteries of the night, a person baptized
by rain and hands of wild grass.

The Great River

Go see [the water ouzel] and love him, and through him as through a window look into Nature's warm heart.

—John Muir, *Our National Parks*

Early one morning in May I step aboard a Greyhound bus in Oakland. A Mexican nun clothed in white and a bald monk from Thailand wrapped in a saffron robe have already settled into their seats. It seems we are all on journeys seeking what we have yet to find. When John Muir first made this trip in 1868, he walked the two hundred miles from Oakland across California and followed the river in. I don't have that kind of time, and the walk is no longer so scenic. The miles of colorful wildflowers that once flourished in the great Central Valley and so impressed Muir have been parceled into huge single-crop farms. Yet the eight-hour bus ride will force me to slow down and move at nature's more leisurely, sauntering pace. The time will also help me set aside the thoughts of deadlines at work that continue to rush through my head like a freight train without brakes.

Instead of packing a car with something to withstand every possible weather condition, I'm carrying only what is definitely needed: tent, sleeping bag, and backpack of gear. There is nothing for just in case, and nothing that will distract me from paying attention to the valley, not even the guidebooks. I want to move from the pleasant and predictable middle earth where I live to a place where I can wake up each day excited about the unknown about to happen.

Arriving in the afternoon, I find Yosemite dissolving. What was frozen over winter is turning into mush—the meadows, the ice-caked mounds of leaves, and the dozen deer tracks preserved in hardened mud. Heavy rains are melting the snowpack in prodigious amounts and streams are rushing down the canyons. Cascades pour over canyon walls every quarter mile, and waterfalls roar as they shoot out into space before crashing down on boulders four thousand feet below, sending hikers scrambling for safety. New creeks form every hour and run over the trails, soaking me up to my knees in icy water as I hike around the valley to see the wild displays. Rivers and creeks surge over their banks and push into low-lying areas, expanding ponds into small lakes and leaving trees surrounded by water wondering where on earth the earth went. Redwing blackbirds trill "ok-ka-lay" over the newly sodden meadows, perhaps reviving ancestral memories from a thousand years ago when this was a wetter place. Mist climbs slowly like koala bears through the branches of trees clinging to the steep valley walls. Rain finds an opening under my hat and drips down my back, but as I slop and slog along the muddy paths I smell the light, sweet scent of Dogwood blossoms and think that this isn't so bad.

New leaves are responding to nature's drive, too, and push through the hard, brown plugs on the end of branches. The yellow-green tips of alders, mountain hemlocks, and willows lighten winter's subdued brown and gray motif. Seeds buried last year in the fall begin to rise from the earth. As another shower tapers off, the rain turns to fog above seven thousand feet and rings the valley in a halo of white. The dark, flat clouds that have dropped so much water move over the horizon leaving scattered cumuli behind.

❧

After a long winter, and with all the melting snow from April, the valley's tiny chloroplast engines cough into high gear. Shoots and tendrils push through the dark earth from some blind clue to unfurl in the air, creating a springtime carpet of tender green that radiates with the sun's warmth. Plants rise with moustaches of dirt and fling swatches of color out like a happy Jackson Pollock. Even pine trees look fresh in their new shades of green. The small flowers on western azalea dot the landscape with thousands of white spots. On the far side of Leidig Meadow, near an intense patch of blue lupine, three purple irises stand regal on long stalks. In the wetter areas I bend down and see the new leaves of milk-weed plants all balled up like tiny geodesic domes ready to pop open and unfold. A mile above me, Yosemite Falls thunders as though a bundle of logs or a gaggle of boulders is going over the top, yet nothing comes down but more water.

I wait for Yosemite to show me what it wants, continuing to find it hard to set my plans aside and stop hiking so fast in my drive to see everything. I'm still full of questions, still wandering around wondering why the river scene at Happy Isles moves me more than the meadow at Mirror Lake, still trying to perceive the valley's different personalities. Each landscape is populated by its own combination of plants and creatures.

On a bend of the Merced River near Rixon's Pinnacle, North Dome and Half Dome reflect off the smooth water. I sit in the quiet of the glen wondering when something, some insight, some breakthrough, is going to happen. The Merced River surges by in a continual flow as it goes on to the farmlands of the Central Valley. In Mesopotamia, life was seen as a journey down a river, moving from life to death. In India, water comes from God's temple in the mountains and flows through Benares in the Ganges River, carrying the dead home. I toss a leaf onto the river for my grief and watch today's allotment float away.

The Sierra Nevada surrounds the valley protectively. For the ancient Greek and Chinese, the tops of mountains were the places where the pantheon of gods and the Immortals lived. The Japanese honored their gods by hiking up mountains and paying their respects to the nature spirits along the way. In the Alps, people for a long time didn't know whether the mountains and forests were filled with dragons or were the artwork of an Almighty Designer. It's not recorded what the mountains thought of them. The taiga forests in Siberia held fears of vicious wild beasts. In the traditions of Judaism, Islam, and Christianity, mountain peaks like Horeb, Carmel, Moriah, and later the Sangre de Christo Mountains of New Mexico were places of epiphany where humans met God and lives were transformed. I toss a stick into the water with my questions, and the river carries them away.

The Ahwahnechees loved this valley and believed that holy beings lived in the mountains, spirits like Tissiack, whose home was in Half Dome and who was responsible for bringing the rains that filled the rivers and nurtured the fish and oak trees crucial to the tribe's survival. I toss a stone into the river and it sinks to the bottom. Like it, I'm not leaving here until I taste life's marrow. A mallard paddles just fast enough on the moving river to hold its position, eating bugs that float down toward it on the surface of the water, and I realize that the river not only carries away what has died but it also brings life to those who wait.

Along these banks there's a deep sense of peace, yet it coexists with terror. No matter how sedate the river may appear, it's as wild as the other creatures of the valley. Strong currents run underneath the surface. If I were to jump in, the snowmelt cold would induce hypothermia within minutes and, with a little more volume, this calm-looking river would sweep me to my death. People have drowned when it's looked quiet like this, trying to wade across. Someone did last year, and Sadie Schaeffer, who's buried in the Pioneer Cemetery, died doing that more than a hundred years ago just a short way downriver toward El Capitan. Nature doesn't stop and make exceptions for people who get in its way.

People die tragically all the time in the valley. Every year climbers are seriously injured and some of them die. But this is a risk that climbers know about ahead of time and accept. Sometimes I think that only the naked fool is alive, the one who dances away at the top of a waterfall while the storm rages about with lightning flashing through the sky and thunder booming and rattling its presence through the bones of every living thing. Yet how long can the fool last before being zapped in the course of nature's events, or being blown into oblivion by a lightning strike? Maybe how long doesn't matter because the goal is to connect to the Spirit of life. The fool and the rock climber understand this but are willing to risk all they have for a chance to participate in the adventure. They accept death as part of life, and this frees them to balance on the edge between calculated risk and logic-defying action as they seek visions of the meaning that lies beyond and within. They are the ones who are alive.

Thinking about this on the way to Degnan's store to replenish hiking supplies, I hear the sound of beaver tails slapping a river. At a table outside, a wild discussion in sign language is flying between four people. What is it like not being able to hear nature?

For me, the auditory experience of Yosemite is important—the roar of waterfalls, the trickle of creeks skimming over rocks, birds and squirrels chirping away, the wind brushing past millions of sugar pine needles and making them hum. The shriek of a Steller's jay, though, is one sound that wouldn't be missed. The sound I value the most is Yosemite's quietness, its lack of noise. It's a refuge from life in the city where every sound crowds in upon the next, demanding to be heard. The resulting din numbs my ear and trains me not to listen to what's going on around me. After arriving in the valley, it takes a day or two for my hearing to calm before I can hear its softer sounds.

A world of quiet is what the deaf always hear. This shifts Yosemite to being a land of the other senses. The deaf do not hear the edges of words that provide clues to understanding the message beneath what is said. They do not hear the emotion in a robin's song or the waterfalls echoing off the valley walls. Without hearing, they have to pay more attention to what is visually going on around them because there are no auditory clues to tell them that a bird is singing nearby or someone is walking behind them. They become attuned to tiny movements in the trees that turn out to be birds, movements perhaps invisible to those who rely on their hearing to help interpret the environment. They see subtle shadings of color that everyone but an artist would miss. And if the eyes of animals and simple organisms can pick up wavelengths of light invisible to the human eye, then who's to say that the sharpening of sight in the deaf doesn't also widen the range of light they see?

Also heightened is an appreciation of touch. No, I think it's more than this. It's a need to touch in order to learn, a desire to know how things feel. Those who walk around barefooted know what the earth feels like, while I, who wear shoes, know what my shoes feel like. The Ahwahnechees were wise to this. If

I valued touch more, I would learn how to tell grasses apart and identify the makeup of soil by the grit. I would be running up to trees and feeling their bark, learning through my hands that this tree not only has rough skin while another is as smooth as a beloved's cheek, but perhaps why. Smell would become more than icing on the cake of my visual experience. It could become the experience, as when my nose lingers an inch from the trunk of a Jeffrey pine and detects a vanilla scent, although some people might be convinced that a pineapple is hiding inside. Besides looking at their cones, whose points either prick me or don't, smelling is one of the few ways to tell a Jeffrey pine apart from its close cousin, the ponderosa, which has no distinctive scent. By tasting some things, and touching, smelling, and looking at everything else, I uncover more dimensions of the natural world and come to appreciate the sensory differences between smooth granite and staghorn lichen, horsetail tips and wet bark chips, green fern moss and the shiny gloss on newly hatched acorns.

The American dipper, a bird that Muir loved, encounters its world as one who is deaf, wanting to stay in physical contact with the river by diving, tossing water on its back, swimming with its wings under water, and bouncing up and down in the rapids to take full measure of its buoyancy. Birds are tactile creatures anyway, flying through streams of air, immersed in the water of the sky's river, and surfing waves of convection that flow over the Sierra Nevada. Climbers hear the rock talk through their bodies, see the stories told in flakes and blocks of granite, perceive its moods and feelings through their legs and knees, and trace the genealogy of the rock's ancestors with fingertips inserted into the stone's cracks and veins. The gear piled around the table indicates that these deaf people are climbers, but how do they tell if the climber coming up last is in trouble?

⮧

One of the aspects I like about Yosemite is that it's a self-sustaining ecosystem. Everything the park needs to survive is here. Every creature in the valley has found a place to exist, not in harmony, perhaps, because everything has to eat, but in balance. There is death happening all around me, but there is also the ongoing renewal of life.

Manzanita bushes illustrate the intricacy of this balance of interdependence. Manzanita has long fascinated me by the way its red branches grow alongside seemingly dead, gray wood. The Ahwahnechees made tea from manzanita berries and bears ate them in the fall. There are seven varieties of manzanita in Yosemite, each growing at a different elevation. The greenleaf variety lives on the valley floor, often as a companion to ponderosa pines. The pinemat manzanita is found at a higher elevation and prefers the company of lodgepole pines. The Ione manzanita has an extremely narrow range, growing only on the few spots that have acidic clay soil, like in the high Sierra by Carson Pass. In an odd twist of coincidence, there also happens to be seven species of warblers in Yosemite. Each lives in its own particular territory and eats its own kind of food.

The oak tree provides a detailed example of how closely life in the valley is interconnected, not just as checks and balances but also as support. At the root level live fungi and termites. Beetles eat the fungi and moles eat the termites. Lizards eat the beetles, gopher snakes eat the moles. (They might eat the lizards, too, if they are hungry enough.) Acorn woodpeckers and squirrels eat the acorns. In the trunk and branches live insects. Red-shafted flickers and Steller's jays eat the insects, while owls and hawks eat the squirrels, birds, and snakes. Mistletoe lives off the tree, and fleas and ticks nibble on the birds and squirrels.

At sunset, after a day of walking around listening to chickadees, waterfalls, and creeks, enjoying the rich, earthy musk of wet land and damp leaves, I lean back against a tree and watch Sentinel Rock's face change from yellow to red, trying not to think of all the animal and insect activity going on behind, below, and above me. Birds close out the day by singing their evening songs. Evelyn once sang Compline, the evening office, in Grace Cathedral, slipping her shoes off so that she would feel grounded. She also slowed the pace of her singing and waited for the echo in the rafters to respond before she sang the next line.

As evening settles over the mountains, climbers and hikers return home from their adventures, light fires in their campsites around the valley that glow in the dark like votives in a great sanctuary, and offer thanks for what today has been. Sometimes I long for night to come because then I have to stop hiking. During the day the continual discovery of new sights and sounds impels me to keep moving and squeeze in another short hike so that I won't miss any stunning scenery or pivotal encounters with nature, even though blisters develop on my feet and my city legs cramp. Without darkness I'd probably keep hiking until I fell asleep on the trail and wake up to find a coyote sitting next to me, watching with curiosity. Tonight's no different as I stiffly get up from my tree, and with a slight limp, join the line of weary, happy people trudging back across the meadow toward camp.

In the middle of the night the roof of my tent lights up as if a forest fire is sweeping through the valley. I throw the tent flaps open and look outside. No fire is visible, but the ferns are glowing and odd shadows are slipping through the forest. I bundle up, head for the meadow, and discover that the full moon is lighting up the entire valley, making it look like the negative of a photograph by Ansel Adams. Everything is reversed, familiar yet different, as if I had been set down twenty-five miles away in Hetch Hetchy, Yosemite's twin valley. The moon's light illuminates every ridge of stone and every rocky point and arch, while the crevices between them stay hidden in the dark.

During the day every part of the valley wall is lit up in bright sunlight and its distinctions are flattened out. In moonlight like this the complexity of the rock can be seen. The walls become massive 3-D swirls of emotion, the anguish and tensions of eons ago caught in this pose when the hot magma suddenly cooled after being in the warm, dark belly of Mother Earth. The black and white scratchboard prints of the mountains created by Jane Gyer, a valley artist, have this same feeling in them, of the earth in flux and being shoved against rocks of different minerals and densities, of melting together, breaking down, and reforming. Yet with all of this physical turmoil, the joy of creation is also here, the ecstasy of the Creator discovering new possibilities and shouting, "Yes!"

Like a cool, barren moonscape, the valley has been recast by the moon's light into gray and black tones and the sheath of physical reality has dissolved. Water in Yosemite Falls stops falling in midair. Oak trees crouch and tell stories of archaic days to the young ferns at their feet. Mountain lions, bears, and owls prowl the edges of the meadows, keeping to the shadows. This is their prime hunting time, and the thought unsettles me. I stay put for as long as I can handle the growing tension, not knowing if they will lunge and bite my thigh or the back of my neck, unable to distinguish me from the deer. As I head back to camp I talk out loud so that they know I'm here. I still fear the terror of the primeval that lingers in the genes of animals, of savagery barely held in check by passing familiarity with humans.

North Rim Trail

In the morning I gird my belt and mental loins and leave camp at 5:30 a.m., aiming to hike the North Rim Trail and immerse myself in the highlands, a twelve-hour, twenty-mile trip that will climb to an elevation of 8,500 feet. I leave camp while it's still dark so that the journey will start out as cool as possible. Temperatures are expected to rise to the eighties in the valley, which is as high as I want it to go on any hiking day. At the trailhead I realize that it's too dark to see which way the trail is going and return to my tent for a flashlight. Back on the trail, my nose begins to hurt. One of the nose rests on my glasses has fallen off and the metal frame is poking me. I head back to my tent, checking the ground with the flashlight.

Inside the tent, I carefully examine the top of everything, hoping the nose rest has simply fallen off. It hasn't. I look around the area where I assembled my backpack, then in my backpack, then everywhere else. The light in the sky begins to brighten. Now I'm throwing things around the tent hoping to knock the pad loose and to the floor, trying not to curse or make any noise because I don't want to wake the climbers in the tent next door. Still nothing. I sit for a moment to calm down, then clear one corner of the tent and systematically look through each item as I move it from one side to the other. Still nothing. I must decide to start the hike now or give it up for the day because there won't be enough daylight to complete it. Maybe something can function as a replacement. I find a finger bandage, cut around the soft pad so that the sticky part will hold it to the frame of the glasses, and start off on the hike for a third time. Now it's light enough that I no longer need the flashlight and leave it behind.

After an hour along the trail that winds up the steep canyon wall, my shirt begins moving to the beat of my heart. This can't be a good thing. I stop to rest on a bend with an overview of the valley, bracing myself against a tree so I don't tumble down the wall. Sitting here, I feel a stirring that I don't recognize, something that finds expression in this outdoor setting, something that feels whole. Taking out my notepad to write about this awareness, I discover the nose rest in its pages. The day is instantly brighter, but forgotten is what I was going to write. I simply jot down, "Something important happened on the bend."

The valley floor is visible between my feet and the buildings and trees look so tiny, two thousand feet away, that I feel like reaching down and moving them around as if they were children's toys. I begin to have additional silly thoughts, but remembering that wisdom often begins with folly, I follow them to see where they lead. "What is the meaning of these trees?" "Why are they here?" Then the revelation comes, after years of searching: the trees are not the question. They never were the question. They are the answer, and I am humbled by my blindness to the obvious. The trees are here because they are part of an evolutionary process. The questions I've really been asking are, Why am I so drawn to nature? Why do I exist? And, of course, the big one, What is the purpose of life? One day I may understand more. Yet I also may not, and that is okay because I'm beginning to understand that life is to be lived as an adventure. I should experience everything I can on the journey, with mystery and heart-shaking challenges stirred in to force me to grow yet keep me humble.

Because of the early start, and with the cool air keeping me from overheating, I make it to the rim of the valley in two hours and feel in decent shape. Had I not felt good at this point, I would have needed to stop because there's no turning back further on. There is no other trail down, no shortcut home. One hundred yards upstream from the Upper Fall the trail crosses Yosemite Creek on a brown thickly hewn wooden bridge. A small valley cradles the creek in a scene of loosely spaced green trees, and the gray granite stonework of the trail leading out of the basin is detailed and exquisite. Hiking up the steep canyon toward the ridge on the other side, I stop at Yosemite Point and look down at the top of Lost Arrow. It doesn't quite come up to the edge, its top having eroded away over the centuries. No climbers are doing a Tyrolean traverse to it today.

THE LOST ARROW LEGEND

Koossokah was set to marry Teeheenay. He went hunting above Yosemite Falls for the wedding feast, and was to drop an arrow from the top of the cliff to indicate how successful he had been. Finding no sign by the end of the day, Teeheenay climbed to the top, looked down, and saw Koossokah's body on the rocks below. When his body was brought up, she embraced him and her spirit joined his. The arrow was never found, but in that spot a granite shaft rose that looks like an arrow.

Once over the ridge, the trail slopes down toward Lehamite Creek near the top of Indian Canyon. The Ahwahnechees made the shafts of their arrows from the mock orange bush in this area. The second year's growth grew straight with a lightweight center that allowed arrows to fly great distances. Indian Canyon is the route the Natives used to make it to the rim of the valley, hence its name. It's also the path Muir and the early settlers first hiked up. There was no Yosemite Falls Trail then.

On the rolling trail between Lehamite and Royal Arch Creeks, after hours of strenuous hiking, I slide into a steady saunter through the idyllic shade beneath white firs and Jeffrey pines, warming up on the gentle ascents and cooling down on descents that are gradual. The mid-sixty degree temperature is perfect. I'm cruising over the trail, throwing my legs ahead of me, swinging my arms and pushing off with my toes, exhilarated by the aerobic exercise. After ten minutes of flowing along the trail, I begin to wonder why I haven't seen any other hikers. This makes me think that wild animals are prowling around and I shouldn't be hiking here alone. I feel a presence and slow down, then stop and look to see what is causing this sensation.

This area is completely in the shade and under a thick canopy of trees, spacious with no brush underneath. Overhead a roof of illuminated green leaves is providing a diffused light on the trunks of hundreds of trees standing like pillars holding up a great roof. It's a natural sanctuary. On the far side are a great stone wall and the chancel. I'm standing in the narthex looking in. It has a spacious feel, filled with cool forest smells and the hushed sounds of a protected glen.

After ten minutes the urge to resume hiking begins. I don't want to leave this cathedral of the wild but I'm five hours along on the hike with at least seven hours to go, and I don't know if I'm even physically able to finish a trip this demanding. The margin for error seems slim, especially if I twist an ankle or wander off on a wrong trail. Reluctantly, I leave.

Approaching North Dome, I emerge from the cool protection of the trees onto the bare rock of Indian Ridge and out into the hot bright sun and the rarefied air of 7,500 feet. I climb down the unstable spur trail and walk out on top of imposing North Dome. The entire valley opens up around me. North Dome sits on the middle bend of the Y-shaped valley. Tenaya Canyon comes in on the left. The Merced Canyon is across the way, and the main

Yosemite Valley stretches off to the right. I look for trails I've hiked and notice how well they follow the contours of the terrain. This was one of Muir's favorite places to sit and reflect. Under my shoes I feel the massive power that pushed this dome up thousands of feet through the earth's layers and into the sky, and imagine Muir standing beside me, looking fondly at his glaciers in the distance. I imagine the Ahwahnechees standing here, watching their beloved eagles soar over the land, and all the hikers, too, who have stood here over the years and felt the glory of nature rise up and pierce their hearts with wonder.

Although glaciers took away the softer rock from the sides of North Dome, the dome doesn't seem less because of it. The stripping away of the excess revealed its strengths, its muscles and sinews, which may be why I feel so alive in the park. It's as if there was a glacier at the El Portal entrance to the valley that scrapes off everyday concerns when I enter, leaving me feeling naked and exposed. This renews an idea that started when I was watching the deaf group yesterday, one that I probably wouldn't do if I thought too long about it.

Taking off my clothes, I sit crossed-legged on the summit, close my eyes, and let the sun warm my skin, feeling the spirituality of the place. There are no sounds except the wind guiding my thoughts. I am Lizard, baking on the rock, touching the warm stone with the skin of my legs until I am the same temperature. I am Bird, flying high in the breeze, sweeping over North Dome, down into the valley, and up to Glacier Point, banking left on the current flowing over Half Dome and feeling the texture of the air as it flows over my wings, breathing it into the hollow of my bones. I let my senses flow.

Then grit kicked up by the wind gets in my mouth, a cloud moving in front of the sun turns the air cold, and the thought that a mother mountain lion is training her cub to attack a human sitting alone makes me turn around. The feeling of connection ends.

As I'm putting my clothes back on, the luscious scent of an unknown flower floats by. I hop down the left side of the dome in search of its source, wishing I had pulled my pants up or at least tied my shoes. The side of North Dome is scattered with pebbles and there is nothing to save me if I trip on a shoelace or slip on a piece of gravel. I stop moving and try to steady my balance in the stiff wind. Muir once slipped and hit his head and knocked himself out on Mount Watkins, a little further back in this canyon. When he came to, only a few small bushes were holding his body from rolling over a thousand-foot drop. There are no bushes here for me to grab, no rocky ledge or tree that would stop my rolling body. I'm on a rounded dome on the edge of a canyon wall. Yet since I'm this far forward, I hold my pause a moment longer and look for a way down to Washington Column. It's a long, rocky slide. More important, I see no way of scrambling back up a thousand feet of smooth granite.

Backing away from the edge carefully, I finish dressing and begin the climb up the long, steep grade of Indian Ridge that rises a thousand feet higher than North Dome. Under a pine tree halfway up the ridge I take a much-needed break to catch my breath, hiding from the sun in the tree's shade and taking my backpack off. The welcomed breeze cools the wet shirt on my heated back.

I continue up a more gradual incline, make a side trip to the Indian Arch, and start on a long downslope until I reach Snow Creek and the cool air of the forest. This section of the river looks like the Fallingwater design of Frank Lloyd Wright: large rectangular stone slabs running horizontally across. Under the deep green shade of the mature forest I pull my shoes off and submerge abused, hot feet in the house's sparkling cascade, eating a belated lunch on its veranda. John Muir took very little food with him on his jaunts through the mountains as he connected with the spirit of the land, sleeping on pine boughs he cut down. He wouldn't do that anymore, knowing that if millions of hikers did that each year, forests like these would be destroyed. Sunlight filters through the trees onto boulders the size of houses lining the brown riverbank, the water having worn away the softer earth between.

On the far side of the dark forest the silvery, glacier-polished eastern wall of Tenaya Canyon rises up in front of me and a shining wave of heat blasts me in the face. The afternoon sun is using the opposite wall, from Half Dome past Clouds Rest, as a reflector oven that is baking my side of the valley. I begin hiking down the switchbacks into Tenaya Canyon, wiping away the sweat running into my eyes and swishing flies that want to buzz inside my nose. I try to use my awe of the earth's geology, exposed in swirls of stone six thousand feet high and many miles wide, to distract from the trauma my body is going through. A couple of times I lose focus, forget where I am, trip on loose rocks and tree roots growing over the steep trail, and almost stumble over the edge. I make one quick stop to place bandages over blisters that are forming on the tips of my toes as the result of the hours of downward hiking. Near the end I concentrate on moving as quickly as possible to reach the valley floor behind Mirror Lake before it gets dark. I vow never to hike this trail again. Yet the views have left me mute with awe, and there's no other way to see them, so I'll probably come back.

Three hours later, after jogging by Mirror Lake on the flat valley trail, I viscerally know why I love nature so much. In twilight like this, as well as in the half-light of dawn, the eternity of the rocks and the presence of a unifying force are felt. I also feel this when a storm has cleared and sunlight dances with departing clouds, or when fog lingers in the crevices of the valley walls. These scenes move into my heart like the corner of a piece of paper put to a pool of ink, drawing the feared darkness of the wilderness into the light where its mystery adds richness to life.

I realize today that when I go into the mountains to hike, I take my struggles with me, and what I encounter on the trail helps me loosen their knots. Yet when I come back down into the valley, I get caught again in the dreams that have died and I wish for a different future than one that is possible. But as Prof. Dumbledore says in one of the Harry Potter books, "It does not do to dwell on dreams and forget to live."

On the way back to camp my weary legs take me along the Merced River and I surprise a pair of thirsty raccoons on the river-bank. They blink and waddle off into the woods. On the horizon, the moon hangs like an eyelash of white about to open. Twilight changes into night and the deepening darkness of Sentinel Rock looks like the same darkness that is in the ponderosa pine trees to my right. It's also the same darkness that is in the river surging past me with longing on its journey out of the mountains to the great Central Valley and on to the ocean, releasing its evaporation into the sky and its cyclical return to the earth as rain. This darkness is in the shadows that cover my feet, in the folds of my shirt, in the dark creases of my brain. I close my eyes and let this flowing river of darkness take away thoughts of my dead, take away the events of today, and prepare me for the changes of tomorrow. I follow the river flowing through the valley of my shadows into the great eternal depths of night that twinkle with bright stars. Darkness is where the light is born, light that I am beginning to see again.

Where Earth Begins

[W]e are all, in some sense, mountaineers, and going to
the mountains is going home.

—John Muir, *Steep Trails*

Between rain sprinkles in the morning, I spend half an hour talking with Ian near the bear-proof dumpster in Camp 4. He's from
Perth, Australia, in his late twenties, medium-built, with short
hair that is balding on top. He's been traveling with Colin for five
weeks, driving cross-country from New York to California with
climbing stops in Kentucky and Utah. Back home he works in
the mines and deals with the 120-degree summer temperatures
by wearing a hat and drinking a lot of water. He hates the cold
and as it's winter back home, he's come to the warmth of North
America. Colin is taller, about six-foot-two, with blond dreadlocks and a trim goatee. He doesn't like to converse. Ian says the
tallest mountains in Australia are only six thousand feet high, so
Yosemite's fourteen-thousand-foot peaks—and the possibility
of meeting some of the great young climbers like Steph Davis,
Dave Graham, Lisa Rands, and Chris Sharma—have made him
ecstatic. As we talk about the history and personalities of Yosem-

ite's early climbers, Colin fidgets on the side, obviously anxious to go climb something, anything.

When I mention that climbing was a spiritual experience for Royal Robbins and that Yvon Chouinard got mystical on the Salathé Wall, Colin walks away. Ian says there are times when he's climbing that things happen he can't explain, like finding an invisible crack with his fingertips or knowing that a move he just thinks of will work. Sometimes, after days on the rock, his mind begins to play tricks and he hears things. I remember reading that John Salathé, another of the early Yosemite climbers, heard voices when he climbed and once saw angels hovering around him. A few people think the stress got to him and he went mad on the rock.

Mike comes along, loaded down on his way to solo climb the West Coast route of the North American Wall. He keeps to himself most of the time, getting gear ready for the next climb. I allow him his space and don't know much about him. Like me, he's focused on his own search. The section of El Capitan that he's climbing received its name because it looks like a map of North America. This means that he will have to climb it twice, going up one pitch to set new safety gear, then climbing down two pitches to pick up the old. I'm impressed by his ambition. He's impressed, too, but still nervous about the risks of attempting an eight-day climb by himself. Behind us, Larry is trying to convince Jim that he's ready for harder climbs. This morning Jim put a note on the camp bulletin board about a number of routes he wanted to do with an experienced partner. Larry saw it and has been pestering him since. "I'm really mellow on the rock, man. I'm not scared at all. When I'm done, I'm scared, but while I'm on a climb, I'm really focused and willing to lug the gear!" Jim arrived yesterday from Lake Tahoe and isn't convinced enough

to trust his life to this young climber. The accident yesterday—
someone fell while free-climbing Sentinel Rock and had to be
evacuated by helicopter—has made Jim cautious.

Each campsite in Camp 4 holds six people, arranged in the
order in which they arrived. No reservations. In the summer,
people start lining up at the ranger booth at 4:00 a.m., hoping
a spot comes open. There are thirty-seven sites, making a total
of two hundred and twenty-two people living in close proxim-
ity. Most people come alone or in pairs. Foreign groups tend to
stay to themselves, speaking their native French, Italian, Spanish, Japanese, or German. Individual climbers have to interact
more because they need to find other people in order to climb
the big walls.

Yet all is not as peaceful as one might suspect. A new arrival
to my site brought this to my attention. Steve is in his early thirties and says he's a moderately good climber. He also kayaks,
hikes, and fishes in the wilds of Colorado. Right now he's waiting for a friend to finish El Cap, then they're off to do a climb
together. He mentions the ongoing animosity between American
and European climbers because training differs, as well as at-
titudes. The Europeans, he says, pay a lot of money to get here
and they understandably have a specific number of world-class
routes they want to do in a short amount of time. But many of
them don't have the techniques for the big walls. He thinks they
need to practice on smaller walls first because they clog up the
premier routes while working out how to move up sheer walls
that are thousands of feet high with little to hold on to and few
ledges that offer rest. They also tend to use too many long ropes,
which get in the way of groups climbing below them. Some are
a tad haughty, feeling that since Europeans have been climbing
mountains for a lot longer than Americans, they know best how

to climb. Americans correctly say that they pioneered the climbing of big walls, so there's a standoff.

About a fifth of the climbers are female. There's friction there, too. After pointing out with pride that Lynn Hill was the first person to free climb the nose of El Cap, Bridget talks about the lack of respect from some of the male climbers who want women to stay on the minor routes, leaving the main ones for the big boys. I'm not surprised. Sometimes the testosterone level around camp gets pretty high as groups try to out-climb each other, but generally it's a friendly competition that encourages everyone to do better. Yesterday a group of female climbers were talking to each other at a table, complaining about the abuse tossed at them by a few men who felt they were moving too slowly up Cathedral Rocks and taking too many "tea breaks." Bridget is about five-foot-two and her tent is on the other side of camp, so I hadn't met her before, but we fall into easy conversation as I wash my favorite hiking socks in a plastic basin by the bathroom.

Each evening the Camp 4 community gathers around dozens of tribal fires to tell stories of their day's adventure, as well as the failures they're ready to talk about. These communal gatherings are a sharing of encouragement and a renewing of vision. It's facing the fears that people have about climbing a technically difficult route tomorrow.

Walking around camp, I move from darkness into the light of each campfire, listening to people talk about routes, to discussions on ways to climb around specific problems, to the pulling out of maps and the tracing of challenging routes with names like Eagle's Way, Dihedral, Genesis, Moby Dick, and Never Never Land. At one fire the talk is quieter and therapeutic: "When we first got here, I was really worried about you. You were withdrawn and uncommunicative. Now you seem to be doing better."

There is the careful packing of gear, the filling of water bottles, the cutting of hair in the flickering light, the stumbling back into camp of those who just finished long, exhausting, one-day ascents, and the crackling sound of short wave radios making connections with homes half a world away: "The climb was unbelievable! You should have seen the moves I made!" Also there are the thank yous between climbing partners who entrusted their lives to people they met only days ago, who counted on each other's bravery and skills for their survival.

On the other side of camp, thirty people from around the world have gathered at a campfire and are taking turns playing guitars and singing songs from home. It sounds like they also have a mandolin. Lying down in my tent, I listen to the joy of their music far into the night.

In the morning I walk over to an unrestored part of Sentinel Meadow and try to dig myself in, try to get below the surface and plant myself into the earth, force my way into a relationship with the valley by rooting my fingers into the soil. I did this once in a botany class at the University of Wisconsin in Madison. We dug up a square foot of land in the woods by North Hall to see what lived on and in the ground at its various levels, using books to help us identify what we found. Later I learned that Muir had lived in North Hall, scavenging branches from these trees to heat his room in winter, and the hill we were digging in was named in his honor.

Sticking a foot or more above the ground in Yosemite's meadow is a mixture of native bunch grasses, red brome, wild oat, and foxtail fescue. There's a dusty plant with tiny white flowers at the tip that might be Indian hemp. I wouldn't have noticed the flowers had I not been lying flat on the ground and looking at it from a foot away. On the right is some kind of miniature milkweed. Growing one to twelve inches above the ground is turkey mullein, a shoot of bay laurel, and city grass, perhaps the Kentucky variety brought in by early settlers to give them a touch of home. On the ground is a meager layer of partially decomposed meadow litter: leaf pieces, matted dead grass, and a few wood chips. A Steller's jay lands behind me, curious to know what I'm doing, but I ignore its questions. It's better that way.

PLANTS AND TREES

There are fourteen hundred species of flowering plants in Yosemite, spread over seven plant communities, corresponding roughly to every two thousand feet of change in elevation. Because the settlers drained the marshes in the valley, trees moved in and now only 30 percent of the valley is meadow, compared to 60 to 70 percent in the 1850s.

Many of the high Sierra meadows were forested at one time. As the land rose, the climate turned colder, ground water increased, and trees simply drowned. Typically the northern sides of Sierra mountains are heavily forested, with red and white firs growing in abundance. On the southern side, where moisture evaporates more quickly, the land is open and brushy, with Jeffrey pines and huckleberry oaks. The giant sequoia reached Yosemite fifteen million years ago from Idaho, migrating over before the Sierra crest rose to its current height. The sequoia settled in at the five-thousand-to seven-thousand-foot level.

In the dry ground there are holes two centimeters across, but when I excavate them with my stick there are no insects, beetles, ants, or grubs, not in the first inch nor in the five inches down where I reach compacted earth. I was expecting creatures like earthworms, beetles, rotifers, millipedes, or at least the tunnel of a mole. But nothing's here. Apparently every creature that could has migrated closer to the river as this part of the meadow dried out. Now I begin to hit a layer of rocks, and frustrated with what little I'm finding, I go over to the low-lying marsh.

Here I find greater diversity: Macloskey's white violet, daisy fleabane, field mint with its tiny violet flowers, Sierra lessingia with its lavender blossoms, purple lupine, white-flowered yarrow, and an emerging spiral basket plant with a brown seed on top that holds the three dozen arms of the basket together. I pull the seed off and the arms slowly fold out into shape. Tufts of bunch grass stand on dark mud pedestals as if waiting for an ocean wave to bring in fresh nutrients. There's also a star-shaped plant that is called a showy milkweed, a plant with little pea buds, the primrose monkey flower, and a plant shaped like a tiny Buddhist prayer wheel sending prayers flowing over the mountains on the wind. The wheel turns the earth, which turns the seeds in the soil that sprout and become plants. The earth turns and the rains return to Yosemite, to a valley nourished by the fallen husks of dead stars and migrating gods. An ancient people left seeds of wisdom in their mythologies to rise in humanity's memory and explain why life is a cyclical battle against death.

Half Dome Hike

Today's hike is to Half Dome. This is the glory hike in the valley, and there are t-shirts in the gift shop that say, "I Hiked the Dome!" I've resisted going on the trek partially because it was so popular but also out of respect for the Native Americans, who felt that the spirit of Tissiack, the one who brings rain to the valley, lived in the rock. Recently I decided that hiking up would be a way of honoring their beliefs and would make their mythology come alive. Eighteen miles long and climbing to an elevation of 9,000 feet, the hike takes about nine hours. At the top of Nevada Fall I begin playing trail tag with eighteen high school sophomores from Santa Barbara as they head for the top of the Dome. When they take a rest, I push on. When I rest, they catch up. On the pass-throughs I talk with Bryan, their twenty-two-year-old leader, who teaches calculus. When he finds out I'm from Wisconsin, he gushes about Aldo Leopold and how influenced he was by Leopold's book, *A Sand County Almanac*. Muir he respects, but Leopold he adores.

The trail has been mostly uphill until the Little Yosemite Valley turnoff. Now it's completely so, winding through thick forests, which block the views, and up sandy trails with shifting traction that makes the hike laborious. We slog through the growing heat of the day, stop, drink water, begin again. The procession of people hiking up this trail reminds me of pilgrims going up Mount Fuji. Finally we reach the clearing on the right side of Half Dome and look over Tenaya Canyon with its drop of a mile to the valley floor. Across the way I see the North Rim Trail that I had to hurry down in May when daylight was fading. Clouds Rest is to our right and Half Dome to the left, but it's a great deal further away than expected. Bryan has warned me about the next part so theoretically I'm ready for the switchbacks that climb the steep hill of Half Dome's right shoulder. The trail then crosses over the shoulder to the cables that go up the neck to reach the top of Half Dome's head. The switchbacks are steep and the granite steps are hot in the ninety-degree sunshine. The stone burns my skin when I reach down and touch it, wondering if the soles of my shoes are melting. I give thanks for the many thoughts I feel compelled to write down because they provide an excuse to stop and catch my breath.

Finally I'm standing at the bottom of the cables that seem to go straight up the slick rock surface of Half Dome, thinking what most people think when they see them: "You've got to be kidding!" A posted sign warns of the danger of lightning: "If a storm can be seen anywhere in the area, it's time to head down. Static electricity travels well through high altitude air and Half Dome is a great lightning rod." I scan the horizon, then join the line of people beginning the climb, donning a pair of used gloves from the pile provided to deal with the metal cables. In order to move forward I half pull with my arms and half push with my legs, resting on the footboard at each stanchion. We all rest at each stanchion because this is like climbing a one-thousand-foot ladder. The stanchions are eight feet apart, which doesn't seem far, but at this altitude every break is welcomed. Partway up some people panic at how vertical the climb is, how slippery the surface of the fifty-degree-angled rock, and they have to be calmed. One person won't and has to be helped back down. Three people died last year when they lost their grip on the cables and fell. Further on, the bodies of others give out. They rest, struggle a few more feet, then go down. Halfway up, my arms go numb because they're over my head for so long, which makes pulling with them comical. My arms flop over the cables and look like they either have a mind of their own or no mind at all.

Gradually the rock's curve lessens, the cables end, and I let my numb arms fall to get their feeling back. On top I celebrate the 360-degree view of Merced Canyon, Yosemite Valley, Tenaya Canyon, and the eastern ridge of the Sierra that drops down to

Mono Lake. There is nothing higher in this area except Clouds Rest, a mile away and rising a thousand feet higher. The top of Half Dome is the size of a football field with a saddle's dip in the middle. There are about eighty of us milling about. The top isn't as smooth as it looks from the valley floor; it's exfoliating, like the other domes I've been on, with foot-thick sheets of granite skin flaking off because of the tremendous pressure stored in the rock. I hop on one piece in the hope that it might pop and catapult me into the air, but without luck. The front edge of Half Dome's face is layered like scalloped potatoes. Because Evelyn always wanted me to be careful, instead of strolling to the edge of the overhang I slide over and carefully peer down its flat face. A few climbers are below, tacking in lines halfway up. Standing, I borrow Muir's technique and survey the high country for scattered patches of tall trees rising above the forest. These are the groves of giant sequoias.

Over the Sierra crest to the south, a line of clouds is stalking along the edge like mountain lions behind bushes on the hunt, their eyes barely visible above the horizon, making me think that they will soon rise up and pounce on the valley. Rain here in June is rare, but it does happen. However, there's no lightning in the clouds. In the small snowfield that has lingered on into summer I make a snowman of Muir, complete with scraggly beard, then sit with cold John for awhile, eating a snack and savoring the view, feeling connected to Half Dome, Native Americans, and Muir, who was the eighth person up this route.

Drinking a bottle of glacier-filtered water in a place where glaciers carved through solid granite, I realize that Yosemite Valley is half dead. This is said without sadness, though, because I like the broad meadows and they weren't originally here. I toast the valley for what it is now, a place of audacious beauty and mystery.

Then I try to imagine how the valley looked in the time before the meadows filled half the valley, before the glaciers, when the Merced River ran three thousand feet lower and the walls of the valley met on opposite sides of the river. On the walls there are patches of white where flakes of rock dozens of feet wide have broken off, continuing the process of evolution that will eventually fill the valley until it is no more. Yet the spirit of this place will endure. The roots of new trees will reach down through the soil of new meadows and touch the bones of their ancestors. The descendants of today's birds and bears will carry Ahwahnee's grace in their beaks and on their backs. People will continue to come because of what they feel in this mountain place and to honor the power of their ancestors' visions. The life of the valley will endure, no matter what form it takes in the centuries to come.

Sauntering over to Half Dome's left temple, I watch cars in the valley drive around looking like specks. I walk further down the curving granite until my shoes begin losing their grip. Below is the Diving Board, the rocky point where Ansel Adams took his famous photograph of Half Dome's face. I scan the woods looking for a way up Half Dome's neglected shoulder, but it looks like a scramble over treacherous land. Back in the saddle, I take one last look around, spot tiny hikers waving at us from the top of North Dome, wave back, and head for the cables. Going down is easier than coming up, although if my feet aren't at the correct angle on the rock I could still slip into the scenic abyss. Midway down I brace myself against a stanchion and take a photograph, shaking my head over the risk that George Anderson took by climbing up this slick rock more than a hundred years ago. Another Scot like Muir, Anderson balanced on single nails he worked into cracks, dragging a rope behind him as he laid out this route foot by foot. His daring, foolish dream became a gift and a challenge to others. Looking below my feet, down where the cables end, it looks like Half Dome is held up by a shoulder of land, a very slender shoulder that a decent-sized earthquake could crack.

Today's adventure reminds me of the challenges that frequently appear in Joseph Campbell's mythological stories: "So, human, you want to reach the sacred place? Let's test your resolve. First, let's see if you can get up the slippery steps and chilled spray of the dangerous Mist Trail to Vernal Fall. Now let's try your legs on the endless switchbacks to Nevada Fall. Then hike uphill through sand and heat for two hours. You think your next challenge will be the cables? Wrong! Now you have to climb the Steep Staircase for half an hour, with each stair being the height of two steps, in bright, hot sun, blowing wind, and nothing to grab if you slip or pass out. This you must do at an elevation of eight thousand feet. Then, and only then, if you make it that far and can still stand, you have the privilege of taking the test of the Dreaded Cables That Go Straight Up. But if you fall there, human, you fall forever. Ha! Ha! Ha!"

The hike back is steadily and sharply downhill for nine miles. At one of my rest stops a pileated woodpecker peeks out from behind a tree to see what I am. A gangly bird, eighteen inches long and skinny, it looks like an anorexic crow with red, white, and black colors. It hops up the backside of the tree, alternately poking its head around the trunk to keep tabs on me. Further down the trail, now bored with mile after mile of nothing to see on a path closed in by trees, my mind starts creating dozens of maxims that seem tremendously profound. Four of them still make sense when read later:

> When I'm tired of hiking and lifting my legs becomes a chore, I try to decide which side of the trail is lower and

requires less energy. The difference of even an inch makes a big psychological difference.

A wide-brim hat amplifies the sounds of streams and birds, helping me hear more of what is around me. It also amplifies the sound of my backpack rubbing against my clothes, making me think that bears are sneaking up behind me.

If water tastes really good on a hike, then I'm dehydrated and need to drink a lot more.

A trail can be considered steep if, while descending, I pick up my back foot and it swings to the front on its own.

At Nevada Fall I take a long break at a familiar spot under the trees by the river, grateful for the cool breeze. I pull off my shoes and stretch out on the flat rock to gaze at Liberty Cap. There are so many fracture joints crossing Liberty that it's amazing the glaciers didn't simply break it into pieces and carry it away. Once again a red-tailed hawk glides overhead. I like thinking it's the same hawk that flies over whenever I take a break, like an old friend coming by to say hello. This hawk is as eternal as the durable rock that makes up Half Dome; something within this bird harkens back millennia and is passed on to each new generation.

One day Evelyn sat here. Before then, every time we tried to hike up, the back of her knees would give out by the time we reached Vernal Fall. With tears in her eyes we'd turn around and limp back down. Finally we rented mules and rode all the way up. Ev was ecstatic. She oohed and aahed over the views of the canyon and the backside of Half Dome, thankful to see what I had been describing for so long. She climbed around the waterfall for an hour, taking pictures and grinning with delight. It was warm that day, too, with a cool breeze coming up the canyon as we ate lunch where I now sit.

On the way down from Nevada Fall I catch up to four Amish youth decked out in traditional garb. They look out of place in their black clothes, straw hats, and white caps. I've only seen Amish and Mennonite believers in farm country, so I ask. They say they've come because Yosemite's simplicity speaks to them. They like its directness, its clarity of voice. When the trail moves under the trees, I take my hat off, feeling that Yosemite's forests are holy places. On the brief patch of level ground halfway between the two falls I explore where Snow's Hotel stood 130 years ago, hoping that remnants scattered in the dirt—nails, pieces of carved wood, broken glass from old bottles—can tell me something of the hotel's story, but nothing is left. I stand where I estimate the porch would have been and imagine people coming out after dinner to sit in chairs and listen to waterfalls cascading on both sides of them.

Late in the afternoon I'm back on the valley floor and tempted to let the sacred sweat of Half Dome stay on me for a few days. I'm camping alone so the only one I don't want to offend is me, but after catching a whiff of myself when the breeze turns, I grab clean clothes and head for the shower.

With a few hours of daylight left I walk over to the ranger station to research owls, hoping to find the information to guide my search. I haven't seen a single one and I'm tired of staring at every old tree to see if an owl is hiding there. The literature says there are eight species of owl in Yosemite, and each owl eats a dozen mice a day, typically between 1:00 and 6:00 a.m. I didn't think there were that many mice. Maybe there aren't that many owls. Among the eight species are the Northern pygmy owl, which is only eight inches tall, and the Snowy owl, whose hoot is low like a foghorn and can be heard seven miles away. Owls tend to be lazy, preferring to take over other birds' nests or just laying their eggs in hollow trees. They're also monogamous. For ears they have small holes in their heads, set at different levels. When they turn they are able to locate objects by the difference of perceptions between their ears and eyes. What looks like ears on the Great Horned owl are just tuffs that make the owls seem more ferocious.

Thirty to fifty Great Gray owls make their home in the park, and although some grow to over two feet tall, they weigh only five pounds. Not only do their feathers make them seem heavier, they also make them silent flyers, unheard by their prey until the owls snatch them up with sharp talons. Most owls in Yosemite Park live around Hodgdon Meadow, forty minutes outside the valley, which explains why it's so hard to find one on the valley floor. Coming out of the Ranger Station, I spot a rare Clark's nutcracker sitting in a tree in plain view of everyone.

At dusk, still charged up from my glorious hike, with muscles growing stiffer by the hour as the physical effects settle in, I straggle to Sentinel Bridge to watch the sunset and plop down on the concrete, stretch my abused legs, and drink more water. I try to massage the kinks out but yelp as I do, glancing around to see if anyone noticed. Two coyotes cross the bridge in front of me on the other side of the one-way road ten feet away. The second one looks back with an expression that says, "Ha! We got across before you saw us." My look says, "Yeah, but you're going the wrong way."

I head for the fir trees in Cook's Meadow. The circular grove is on the edge where there are plenty of mice, and the Merced River is only a few paces away. This should be prime owl territory.

I hear a hoot and jump up, scan the trees, see nothing, and settle back down, trying to move only my eyes. Five minutes later a doe and her fawn come out of the tall grass on one side of the clearing, nibble the shorter grass in the circle, and disappear into the other side, completely unmindful of me. I listen to the tall trees creak overhead as they sway in the breeze, to the light rasp of long stalks of grass brushing against each other, to the casual evening chatter of birds and the gurgling of the river, hoping to hear the one specific sound that will make an owl take flight and search for food. After a time of seeing nothing, I change venues and walk quietly through the shoulder-high grass of Sentinel Meadow, watching the sky and trees for owly shapes and hoping there are no coyotes waiting to nip my heels.

Giving up, I sit on a fence by the road near the chapel, resigning myself to watching the golden fire of the sunset flow over the mountain peaks as night settles in. A large bird flies to the top of a twenty-foot tree across the meadow, swoops to the ground, and is hidden for half a minute as it deals with something in the tall grass that shudders. Then it flies to a branch over the road where I see it silhouetted by Half Dome glowing in the sunset behind it. A Great Gray! When the sunset fades, the owl renews its slow, powerful flight, looking for more mice to eat.

Dissolving the Boundaries

Nature is ever at work building and pulling down, creating
and destroying, keeping everything whirling and flowing.

—John Muir, *Our National Parks*

The middle of summer brings hot temperatures that steep the
mountain's stone, a persistent heat that lingers far into the night
and radiates up from the earth beneath the tent, delaying much
needed sleep. Rambunctious thunderstorms, caught in the unsettled air between warm and cold fronts, boil up and sweep
through the valley in a matter of hours, sending wind and rain
that swirl leaves and small branches down the trails and turn
placid streams into torrents. Then they are gone.

Camp 4 is buzzing from another accident. Two climbers were
working their way up a wall, one taking the lead and moving higher
while the other stayed below, holding his safety line, when a rockslide broke loose above them. As the lead climber scrambled for
safety, his friend continued to hold the line until his partner was
out of the way, but the falling rocks killed him. A number of the
younger climbers are shaken and finding excuses to repair their
gear. The veterans have faced this reality over the years when ropes

snapped, safety clips pulled loose, or rocks crumbled in their hands and sent them falling. Friends also have died from hypothermia because they could not get out of the way of freezing water flowing over the top of El Cap. The veterans shoulder their gear and head out for the walls, a little more somber and careful.

At sunset I amble down to the river in Leidig Meadow. Jupiter rises bright on the horizon. Tonight there's a palpable feeling of something afoot. I feel like Sherlock Holmes looking for telltale signs, trying to discern the cause of my apprehension. What am I not seeing in the small stand of aspen on the bank across the river? I fear that if I don't find the hidden clue, this opportunity will disappear from my consciousness like the colors of the sunset fading from the sky. It's not the beauty that is affecting me but the darkness between the trees. What is in there?

The chirring and chirping of frogs and birds grow louder as the evening's purple light fades. The valley walls shorten as the darkness becomes more encompassing. My small patch of trees pulls back and blends into the mass of trees in the valley. The trees merge with the dark river and the dark meadows, then with the shadowed mountains; everything disappears as night erases the last distinctions in the valley and I see nothing. The only light comes from the stars overhead. Standing alone on a point of the river as its unseen water surges by, in the middle of the valley under a warm evening sky, I face the darkness trying to be open to what it wants to show me. Constellations set. Another group of stars rises and moves to the far side of thought.

Weather has become a companion on my trips, although I seldom know how many clothes it will wear each day. In the mountains the weather changes quickly. Overnight, clouds slip in and look threatening, so I postpone a long hike and pick up one of my contingency plans: a drive to Mono Lake. Above the eight-thousand-foot level the number of trees lessens, revealing more of the bare granite domes and slopes that make up the high country landscape. The first time I saw it I thought it was too stark, too exposed, vulnerable the way a northern town feels in autumn right after the trees have lost all their leaves. I drive higher, into the clouds, until I can see only 100 feet to either side of the road. Olmsted Point, which normally has a grand view down the length of Tenaya Canyon to Half Dome in the distance, is socked in with fog.

The storm clouds darken and the light rain turns into a down-pour that obscures my vision and rivets my attention on the road ahead as I try to anticipate the curves. Tuolumne Meadows is flooded as I stream past. After crossing Tioga Pass at ten thousand feet, the road begins winding down through red slag mountains to Mono Lake, some thirty miles in the distance. This is probably not Muir's Bloody Canyon, named for the injuries that horses suffered on that rough trail, but in this thick deluge, with wind-shield wipers going as fast as they can and tires hydroplaning on the narrow road whenever my speed creeps above twenty miles an hour, the name will do. I slow to a roll, hoping my forward momentum is enough to carry me over the small cascades of broken slate that slide my car toward the canyon's edge.

Mono Lake appears ahead, the rain slows to a drizzle, and I relax my grip on the steering wheel. The area is barren, scraggy with sagebrush and pronghorn antelope. It looks like Nevada with its gray, purple, and burnt magenta colors. Dormant volcano cones, some hundreds of feet tall, dot the landscape and remind of the area's seismic activity. Some of Chief Teneiya's relatives lived here, eating pine nuts and larval grubs and hiking to the valley by way of Tenaya Canyon to trade for game with the valley tribe. The seventy-square-mile lake is serene as it stretches to the Great Basin Desert on the horizon. Dark storm clouds swirl around the edge of the lake as if the water is being held in the eye of a hurricane. It feels like something is about to break.

With one eye on the storm I walk down to the tranquil shoreline, surprised by the sage green and mauve beauty of the land and amazed that the large lake is so still that it reflects the luminous glow of light undulating through the dark clouds. I can hear the ripples washing ashore. Out in the water are the tufas, the white columns of calcium carbonate that form under water. They are visible because of the folly of fifty years of draining the freshwater rivers that feed the saline lake and sending that water to Los Angeles 350 miles away, shifting two ecosystems out of balance, destroying one and artificially supporting the other. With the lake level so low, wolves routinely trot through the shallow water and feast on thousands of baby gulls and snowy plovers. This is one of the primary breeding grounds for seagulls because of the brine shrimp, and it's a migratory stop for many other species of birds.

I turn away from the eerie solitude of the lake, disturbed by the senseless destruction. Looking for where I left the car, a range of brooding mountains looms up before me. Their sharp-crested peaks are hidden in black clouds, and the feeling comes: "Death lives there." I see no light reaching into the depths of the canyons' dark labyrinths, only colors dissolving in gray shadows and the black shapes of ravens and hawks cutting across the sky. If I hiked in there I know that I would not survive. In this moment I realize that the God of nature, whom I thought was so peaceful and benevolent after Sunday's glorious entrance into the sunny beauty of the valley, is also cruel. In this moment my belief in the intrinsic goodness of life ends, like a *Twilight Zone* episode where the curtain of smiles is lifted from people's faces to show their inner thoughts—their greed and anger and hatred and plans of extracting exact revenge on those they think have wronged them.

Blood for blood is the world's code, no matter how I try to dress it up in something more palatable. Survival goes to the fittest. Death to the masses. Forget about redemption or the world progressing and becoming more enlightened. The world will always be what it has been, a dangerous and uncertain place. Now I know that Grimm's Fairy Tales were based on true stories when people did horrible things to each other. I think of the torture inflicted by civilized people in the Tower of London, the Final Solution meted out by the cultured people of Germany, the killing fields of Cambodia, and the ethnic cleansings in Africa, the Baltic States, and too many elsewheres. Human wolves have a long history of causing death when it suits their purpose. I leave the area quickly, wanting to get away from the precipitous despair that is descending on my heart.

At Tenaya Lake I stop to eat lunch and settle my feelings, but I can't concentrate. The beauty and violence of nature have not been so forcibly thrown together for me before. It's like someone has strapped me to a pair of water skis, hooked me to a towrope, and is dragging me away from the safety of the shore called home. I'm clenching the line, afraid of where I'm being pulled but also terrified to let go for fear of tumbling head over heels and sinking into the cold, fluid depths of the wild. I will continue to skim over the surface of the wilderness, ignoring the harsh reality that lies beneath and seeing only the surface beauty, until I break and accept that nature is beyond what I want it to be, until I can let go of the line, sink into the chaos, and surrender to the horror and destruction that seem to be tied to every natural scene of beauty. I thought death was built into life in an organized, purposeful way, but now I feel that death is often capricious, random, and meaningless. Good and loving people like Evelyn just die.

Back in the valley it's still raining. I drive up to the overlook at the parking lot by Inspiration Point and sit on the stone wall. A few tourists stop, snap pictures, and move on. Low rain clouds slide over the valley at the height of the walls, and Bridalveil Fall pours its plume of water into a grove of trees. Patches of white mist rise slowly from the dark pine forests. After an hour of sitting, watching the beauty of this Japanese landscape–like painting shift from one sublime image to the next, and with the drama of the weather seeming to have no end, I head back to camp, cook a sloppy dinner filled with rain, and turn in early. During the night, blustering winds shake the tent and rain pelts the nylon roof a foot above my face. Throughout the night I check the tent for leaks, wondering if my heart is contrite enough to appease the whims of this angry God or if a tree will come crashing down. What is nature trying to teach me?

The storm rages through the night, with driving wind and rain washing away everything that's not tied down and leaving bare, scoured mountains behind. It seems that the doors of the wild have opened and madness has come pouring in. I endure a frail sleep, waking at each flash of lightning and every boom of thunder that echoes off the valley's stone walls.

Valley Floor Perimeter Hike

Dawn opens cold but at least it's no longer raining. Feelings of the brooding, harsh spirit of nature have stayed with me, kept fresh by the rainstorm that pounded my tent during the night. I know that I am not in control here, but now I think that I may not even be safe. I decide to face my unsettledness head-on by walking slowly around the entire perimeter of the valley floor, a total of about twenty-six miles, stopping frequently to look closely at nature and see what examples of death and life can be found. I will also read the Psalms, hoping its words will provide a framework for understanding the trauma going on.

Yesterday's storm has left wisps of low clouds floating between valley walls lit by sunlight, helping me feel a little more hopeful. My saunter begins at Happy Isles on a trail that takes me along the eastern edge of the valley floor. I pass the massive medial moraine of rocks that was left when glaciers came down two different canyons and shoved against each other. The moraine now has trees and a nice view from the top over the length of the valley. I hike through the woods to Snow Creek, go around Mirror Lake, pass the Indian Caves, the Ahwahnee Hotel, Yosemite Falls, and head back to camp. Feeling good and intrigued by the low clouds that continue to linger even though the sun is shining and the sky is a deep blue, I take a shuttle back to Happy Isles and walk the other direction, along the southern perimeter past a flat, thirty-foot-wide rock that I imagine an ancient Indian culture used as an altar for blood sacrifices to appease the gods. I walk by Curry Village, the LeConte Memorial with its native grinding holes, the river bend where Muir liked to watch dippers play, the spot where Black's Hotel used to be with its iron rings still embedded in the boulders to tie up horses, the chapel, and across Leidig Meadow late in the afternoon to my campsite.

I'm halfway around the valley, thirteen miles. There wasn't any consistent reason for the times when I paused to observe and reflect. Sometimes yellow sunlight coming through the green trees created a beautiful scene. Often I lingered by water—a pool reflecting the blue sky, a cascade going over a small group of rocks—and just listened to the sounds. Other stopping places included an old narrow stone bridge that may have been part of the original stagecoach road, and the scene of a forest fire, where a ponderosa pine seedling is managing to grow out of blackened soil.

In the darkness of night the words of the Jewish psalmists come back with their frustrations, anger, and depression. They knew about the dark night when they were weary of trying to hold their lives together, tired of trying to make sense of the chaos, tired of the grief and the injustice that permeated life. They ranted and let God know exactly how they felt. They yelled at the world, at others, even at themselves, because everything they believed and everyone they trusted had failed them in their time of need; they had nothing left. Then, when the light of day broke through the darkness, they sensed enough to believe that there was still some hope.

The next morning opens gorgeous with blue skies, although the dirt trails under the trees are as wet as if it had just rained. Everything is soaked with moisture. The air is so resonant that people can be heard talking across the valley. If the air could be rung like a glass bell, the sound would be clear and true, echoing off the valley walls and coming back with barely a distortion. I walk across Cook's Meadow to the chapel and continue on the trail going along the southern edge of the valley floor, passing Sentinel Dome and Taft Point from a mile below. I see several native grinding rocks along the trail and skirt the base of the Cathedral Spires. The trail rises as it approaches the Cathedral Rocks, and in a short amount of time I'm looking down through the trees onto cars hundreds of feet below driving by. Rubbing the smooth face of the main Cathedral Rock at the point where it rises two thousand feet straight up, my glance goes out across the valley to El Cap and back. I wonder if they were ever connected. It looks like a ridge once ran across the valley and a tremendous act of violence by the glaciers broke it down, enabling a river to flow through and carve this canyon into a valley now filled with an abundance of life.

At the bottom of Bridalveil Fall a heavy, cold mist swirls. The Ahwahnechees believed that bad spirits lived here because an Indian maiden once fell into the creek and died, so they wouldn't camp in this part of the valley. I don't linger, either, but head into the woods to get out of the chilled wind. A huge raven hikes out of the woods and stands near me. The term "huge" may be redundant as these birds are normally two feet tall. Their beaks are thick and powerful, and it's visually obvious why Edgar Allen Poe would put one in his poem as a harbinger of evil and doom. It reminds me of the Great Raven of the Athabascans, who brought to the world the sun and the moon, warmth and light, and who helped people settle the land. This raven doesn't seem to have any malevolent intentions. A coyote limps into our area from the direction of the meadow, lifts its leg and marks a tree stump, then limps back the way it came. The raven and I look at each other and go back to enjoying the quietness under the trees.

After a time, my raven moves on and I resume my hike. I follow the trail through Bridalveil Meadow, with its giant hyssop and St. John's wort, and along the river to Pohono Bridge, being cautious to not disturb any bears hanging out in these seldom-visited woods. The sounds of running water increase as a number of small creeks like the one flowing from Fern Spring join the Merced River. I cross the bridge, where incoming traffic splits from outgoing, and head east along the valley's northern edge, passing on the back side of Black Spring and approaching El Capitan from the left.

Walking by El Cap, I wonder if climbers have rituals that help them feel safe under the eyes of the god of the mountains, like sharing water with the spirit in the rock before climbing each day or pulling three times on a newly placed anchor pin before applying weight. Yet sometimes all their precautions are not enough and climbers fall. I follow the trail back into the heart of the meadow. Yesterday's soaking rain is changing into steam by the iron of today's sun. The sandy soil forces me to slow my pace and the high humidity makes it difficult to breathe.

Ahead of me a coyote is working on something large. Coyotes generally chase mice and voles and chew on them like limp, rubber toys. This is different, so I wait. The coyote spends a considerable amount of time pulling with its teeth at something it's holding down. After the coyote walks off, I approach and see a fawn that's been torn open. That a coyote killed a deer is not a crime, or even a tragedy. Intellectually I know this. But the horror I feel mirrors watching a boyhood friend chopping off the heads of chickens for dinner. In the wild this kind of death is a fact of life. It's the earth turning once and winter wiping out an entire generation of insects and plants. It's the Hindu cycle of endless birth and rebirth, with death mixed in as the key ingredient of transformation. It's standing on your prey's neck and eating while your prey watches, but not paying attention as the light fades from its eyes because if you don't eat quickly, chances are that a stronger predator will come along and either steal your food or eat you too. The deer has died but its body will nourish the lives of others, enabling them to live. Knowing the natural law that energy can neither be created nor destroyed brings some comfort as I also realize that the atoms and molecules that make up my body will continue in some form after I die. Perhaps I will be part of Coyote one day. Maybe molecules of Bear and Raven are already living in me.

Anger over Evelyn's death flows back. I still have not made peace with it. It was not right that Ev should have had to suffer with various illnesses for years and die in her forties after working so hard to get healthy. But after the experiences of the last few days, I know that too many people die before we think it's time, that life is often just plain cruel, and that those who love greatly will also be the ones who suffer most. There are no safe ships that carry us through life, no sanctuaries to protect us from tragedy. We're on our own in this world, so we'd better watch our backs.

One year Muir took his daughter to Arizona to heal because her lungs could not get well in the damp air surrounding San Francisco Bay. While they were there Muir's wife, Libby, took ill. Muir immediately came home but Libby died shortly thereafter, and though Muir tried to keep things going, he began to fade. Then Teddy Roosevelt told his old friend to get into nature and heal. Muir returned to Arizona and slowly recovered over the course of a year. He came back to continue the fight to protect Yosemite. Then politics caused the death of his beloved Hetch Hetchy, which was flooded to provide water to San Francisco even through a better, nondestructive alternative existed, and Muir died a broken man.

Approaching the base of the Three Brothers and Eagle Peak, this humid, clothes dryer of a day makes my mind tumble with images from the last twenty-four hours—deer being eaten alive and dying, the ancient prophets yelling about the abuses of life, climbers risking their lives and dying, Natives eating grub larvae, the wrath of nature, Yosemite's grandeur, Muir's grief, Ev's dying—and my consciousness dissolves and shimmies into space, floating above the land like waves of convection undulating over the meadow. The wilderness, with its great scenes of beauty and uncertainty, is all that I understand about nature but I scarcely comprehend its darkness, or sorrows, struggles, or death. Yet this part is real, too; I can try to run from it, but it won't help. I dip my toes into the world of nature by camping in it for a week at a time, then return home feeling that I have braved and overcome the elements. But some people stay behind, and when I return to the wild for another visit and our paths happen to cross, we scarcely can communicate. They have moved into the unknown, into a relationship with this place, and they have learned of deeper truths.

Sometimes I want to live completely detached from the earth, to do without eating altogether so that I do no violence to any form of life, like the Jains in India who brush insects out of their way. I want to subsist on air, water, and the energy from the sun, even though I know this is impossible. I'd like to carry only flour and tea with me on my hikes, like Muir did. Muir said that we do not know how much uncontrollable there is in us until we ignore our better judgment and go hiking across glaciers and river torrents, where who we are is revealed. Climbers understand this. They take risks in order to stay alive. I want to live in Yosemite authentically, eating what the valley naturally provides—the nuts and berries, bear, deer, and fish—and perhaps be eaten myself, for everything that lives here is a member of the food chain. That's part of the arrangement. The Ahwahnechees believed that the deer they successfully hunted willingly gave their bodies to them to eat and that humans were part of this cycle of life and death.

There are also times when my savageness surfaces, when I want to prowl the forests at night like Thoreau and catch anything that moves, then eat it raw, right then, right there, tearing the warm body of my prey apart with my teeth. This, too, is part of who I am, although I struggle hard to deny its existence. It scares me to think that I would be capable of inflicting such violence

on the innocent, yet I know that I am. I reach the edge of camp
and Psalm 150, the final one, at the same time. It's about praising
God. But I am not at peace with whomever or whatever allows
such violence to happen to the innocent, and I do not read it.
Charles Darwin, when his daughter Annie died, decided to set
his Christian faith aside rather than believe in a God who allowed
such cruelty. He chose instead to believe in the unchanging natural
laws that govern every living creature.

In the morning, Camp 4 is quiet. Even with pots and equipment clanking as people cook breakfast and get ready to climb,
a profound silence pervades the camp. Nicholas is stretched out
reading in his sleeping bag on the open ground. George sits at a
table under the trees, writing in his journal. Others have wandered
down to the river. There's a common need to center oneself before
climbing up a rock wall or hiking into the wilderness, a desire
to deal with one's demons, fears, and feelings of brute savagery.
Whether we hike, climb, or just wander about the valley, our
activities explore the boundaries of self-knowledge. They also
confront the edges of the courage we have in facing our strengths
and weaknesses. At night we are excited about telling the stories
of our great adventures from the day, but in the morning we
know the somber truths about ourselves that have surfaced in
the nightmares of the dark.

The shock of seeing nature's harshness stays with me the rest of
the week, especially the image of the dark, brooding mountains
above Mono Lake. It has shaken the foundation of my beliefs.
If I hiked into those mountains I might not find my way out for
weeks, perhaps years, overwhelmed by the judgment of nature

and perhaps changed into something vicious. If lightning and thunder had been ripping through the sky, or a naked fool had danced about at the top of a waterfall, praising the Creator as the storm raged, I would not have been surprised. The Spirit's home may shine in the beauty of Yosemite but it also lives in the dark valleys and the bloody canyons of terror that run through these mountains. The world's holy scriptures are filled with encounters with divine beings who demand and punish those who fail to measure up. Old Testament prophets repeatedly warned against forgetting to pay proper attention to God, and they detailed how sinners died horribly, torn apart by lions and bears. In the New Testament, God's wrath isn't so much an issue because love is the dominant relationship, but then there is redemptive suffering, where God allows the innocent to suffer, and my thoughts return to Ev and the dead fawn.

After nature's wrath has expended itself, after the great storm that has battered and shaken my resolve has moved on, after the Spirit's angers and passions have cooled and the rain that pounded down has pooled on the trails, there is a period when sweet scents fill the air—the calm after a mountain storm has run its course.

Evening comes on this seventh day and nature glows in the warm, golden hues of a mountain sunset. Two feet above the river a belted kingfisher zips by and sits on a branch to watch for fish. A blue heron flies slowly away barely above the smooth surface of the water. The light of day fades and people and animals turn in for the night. I feel nature's presence in a new way, one that seems to guide and heal. I stand by the river and look again into the darkness of the trees across the river. This time I glimpse a faint movement. I listen for sounds of things to come and hear the river talking and the valley walls antiphonally chanting. I will no longer seek to tame nature as if it were a wild stallion. Instead, I will let nature ride and break me down. I will let myself become part of the cycle of life, death, and transformation. It cannot be otherwise.

Grace collects on the mountain peaks in the high country and flows down the Merced Canyon into the valley as fog, hiding Glacier Point from view. This wet fog moves across Leidig Meadow and overtakes the trees along the river. I breathe it in and smell pine and oak, bay laurel and manzanita. I breathe more slowly and pick up the scents of mountain granite, of Raven and Coyote and the cascades of the high country. Their presence fills my lungs and flows into my body like a river. I feel reverence. The battles with death no longer scare me. As darkness closes off the meadow to sight, the fog continues to flow down the canyon and fill the valley.

Seventh Mountain

> Nearly all my mountaineering has been done on foot, car-
> rying as little as possible ... so I might be light and free to
> go wherever my studies might lead.
>
> —John Muir, *Our National Parks*

Under a dark predawn sky I sit by the pool at the foot of Yosemite Falls, watching stars reflect off the tranquil, black water.
Although Yosemite is the fifth tallest waterfall in the world, the
lack of rain over the summer has reduced it to a mere spout.
One dawn in the 1950s Gary Snyder was inspired by this pool
to write poetry. He was working on Yosemite's trail crew at the
time and later became one of the writers of the Beat Generation.
I want inspiration to strike again and help me accept the tragic
part of life I saw in July.

Water in the Upper Yosemite Fall unfurls like a banner and
drifts onto the breeze toward the Lost Arrow. The basin catches
every stray bit of water and channels it back into the middle section, while Lower Yosemite Fall continues to run steadily down
the face of the rock. Without the heavy rush of spring's snowmelt
roaring down, I can see behind the narrow stream to where the

water has worn a foot-deep groove into the hard granite wall and carved out the basin for this pool.

The chirping of chickadees in the early morning hours and the light schiss of falling water deepen the sense of calm. Summer is beginning to crinkle around the edges. Flowers have retreated to small bogs under groves of trees, hiding from the hot sun. Parental wrens feed seeds to their almost-adult offspring, but the time is near when they will share last meals and go their separate ways. Smells on the dry air have the pungency of sage. I touch water from the pool to my forehead in honor of Snyder, then splash my face and upper body. My skin tingles with its touch.

When dawn breaks into the alcove, I rise and hike the trail to the base of the Upper Fall, two thousand feet higher in elevation. Beyond the Columbia Rock sand field I push through bushes and scramble over boulders to the junction between the Upper Fall and the middle cascades. Just beyond is the Lost Arrow rising out of bedrock. Looking out from the cool of the seven-foot-high cave behind the fall, which looks like a dark grin from the valley floor, I imagine the earth-shaking rumble of being here when the fall was full and roaring down ten feet away. Muir used to climb halfway up Indian Canyon to get here, but that trail no longer exists because of rockslides. Once he spent a night in this cave with a blanket wrapped around him and a single piece of bread to eat.

Only a trickle of water is coming over the cliff, barely enough to run from one small pool to the next, connecting the wet dots. I stand underneath and collect the entire flow of Yosemite Falls in my cup. If I do this long enough the Lower Fall will go completely dry. Setting the first cup aside, I collect another, then turn both cups loose to go flooding down the falls, tripling its output. From here the rock slopes sharply toward the edge of the middle cascades. It's slick from centuries of water polishing the stone surface, but my shoes find enough traction to let me shuffle forward without slipping and becoming part of the falls, like some of those who are buried in the cemetery below. I follow the trail of pools down to the darker rocks.

This middle section has a wildness that reminds me of a landscape painting by Li Huayi. Water runs through a series of steep, narrow chutes with twists and turns that would thrill a mogul skier. Something caught in here would be battered until it was small, or lucky enough, to get through an opening. The trunks of trees are still wedged in its corners and will stay there until next year when the rush of spring's snowmelt sends a torrent of water through. My little flood of two cups apparently didn't free anything. Poised halfway between the valley floor and the top of the canyon wall, a place of turmoil between two scenes of exquisite beauty, every sound is gentle—leaves brushing against each other, squirrels chewing nuts, and little avalanches of gravel that cascade down the slope as chipmunks dig underneath looking for seeds.

El Capitan's Hike of the Hours

First Hour—Vigils. I get up at 3:00 a.m. and eat an energy bar. That's all the food I can handle at this hour. I give quick thanks for surviving the night because bears are prowling the camps again and a mountain lion was spotted behind the horse stables.

Predawn—Lauds. Hitching a ride to the trailhead, I have trouble finding where it starts. In the dark I feel my way along the dirt trail using my hands and feet like a blind man until I find a path that doesn't end in bushes or lead me face-first into a tree. The trail starts along Highway 120 outside the valley, climbs through the mountains, approaches El Capitan from the left, and comes back—twenty-one miles that should take eleven hours. The weather board at the ranger station said today was going to be sunny with temperatures in the low eighties. At the top of the first ridge, with the hope that I'm still on a trail, I see a dim light on the eastern horizon. El Capitan is in silhouette looking small. Mile mark 1.

Dawn—Prime. Am I crazy to be trying this long hike alone, and over unknown territory? What unsocialized animals live here? Finally there's enough light to see the terrain and it's completely open to the sky. A forest fire has killed the trees and bushes have flourished with the increase in sunlight, including some thick strands of bramble that grow over the trail. I ran into them earlier in the dark and struggled to get free, my body caught on three sides like a finger in a Chinese finger trap. On the rise, deer are eating peacefully. I slow down and try to slide past unnoticed, but something startles them and they take off, bounding like big graceful athletes over fallen trees as if they had never seen a human before.

The landscape is unremarkable, with no granite peaks to gawk over, no scenic canyons, and no amazingly huge trees. This is probably why the hiking book recommends this part of the trail for the springtime when there are wildflowers. Hearing rustling, I stop and wait. Another rustle, and a two-foot-long black snake with yellow stripes slides out from under the leaves near my feet. It's not bright red like the king snake, nor are there any rattles on its tail, so it's probably harmless, but it's the biggest nonlethal snake I've ever seen. Thankfully the air is still cool and the snake is moving slowly. Half an hour later the trail brings me to the paired creek canyons of Wildcat and Tamarack that have worn steep creases into the side of the mountain. Mile mark 2. Under the thick canopy of trees little disturbs the seclusion deep in this crevice of the mountain. I push through the brush and crawl fifty feet up the boulders into the green moss-covered channels and listen to water trickling and dripping down the ancient courses.

Midmorning—Terce. Mile mark 4. When I reach Cascade Creek I glance at its small pools and calculate that they might be warm enough on the way back for a delightfully refreshing dip after a sweaty hike. My path joins the Tamarack Trail that comes in from the left and follows the path of the Old Big Oak Flat Road, built for stagecoaches in 1874 and later paved for cars. It was abandoned in 1940 for the present road along the river that is wider, so for a short time my hiking path becomes a luxurious, ten-foot-wide paved trail. A short distance beyond the junction two climbers are sleeping. Hearing me approach, they raise their heads to see how dangerous an animal I might be. They say they made it to the top of El Cap late yesterday then hiked this far in the dark; the trail I want is half a mile down on the left and it's easy to miss. I let them know, to their annoyance, that they still have a fair distance to hike before reaching Highway 120. I continue downhill on the old road, and they go back to sleep.

After going a quarter mile too far I backtrack, find the trailhead hiding in the bushes, and begin a steep climb that will take me up to an elevation of 7,600 feet. Already I can tell that today is going to be warmer than predicted, probably reaching the nineties. Shortly after starting up the trail at my faster downhill pace, my legs feel like kielbasa. I cut my speed in half and plod up the trail through viewless woods, placing one foot in front of the other as I make my way up the mile-long side of the mountain, wondering if any animals are watching and amused that I have to stop so often to catch my breath. I name this section "The Climb of Ten Thousand Steps and One Hundred Stops." When I reach the top of the mountain the trail, which had been easy to follow on the soft, piney ground of the cool forest, emerges into the open and into bright, hot sunlight that glares off the white stone. I'm blinded. I dig sunglasses out and slap on a broad-brimmed hat. Mile mark 6.

Here are several trails heading in different directions, but none are distinct and not one heads east toward El Cap. I make an educated guess, take a deep breath of hot air, and push into the hot glare, feeling like a fish thrown out of the cool ocean and into an oven. I cross the bare rock and head north to follow the sporadic piles of stones called trail ducks left by previous hikers to guide those coming later. I figure this trail is working its way around an unseen canyon. At 11:00 the trail leads me back into the valley with a great view of the south wall. Alleluia! I'm standing thousands of feet above the level of Bridalveil Fall, and looking down on it the fall looks surprisingly tiny. I can also see the huge, polished-rock canyon behind Bridalveil that gathers the fall's water, as well as the massive granite block that makes up the Cathedral Rocks and Spires. On the ground in front of me a family of western fence lizards lounges in the sun, enjoying the warmth after yesterday's cold rain. One lizard is doing morning push-ups. I jump over the water in Ribbon Creek near where it flows over the edge into the canyon, and hop from dry spot to dry spot to get through its muddy meadow. There's enough moisture left here to sustain the flock of butterflies fluttering about. Emerging on the right side of El Capitan, I follow a foot-wide path along the edge then cut up a ridge to the pinnacle.

High Noon—Sext. Mile mark 10.5. Kneeling down, I place my hand on the rock with reverence, scarcely believing that I'm here.

Joy surges and I let out a big yell, trying not to get too giddy be-cause I still have to get back down safely. A large bird—either a peregrine falcon or a goshawk but moving so fast that I can't tell which one it is—shoots through the trees like a miniature jet.

I walk down El Cap's steep sloping forehead until my shoes begin sliding and knocking pebbles loose that roll toward the edge, potentially hitting climbers making their way up the face. Carefully I shuffle sideways to the shade under a large Jeffrey pine. This view rivals what can be seen from the tops of Sentinel, North, and Half Domes. A steady breeze offsets the hot sun and keeps the air cool. Vultures soar gracefully in circles like black paragliders as they ride the thermals for thousands of feet. I hold a memorial service for Stan, my father-in-law who died a few years ago. He loved Yosemite because it affirmed his faith in a God of Majesty, and El Capitan inspired him with its endurance. I build a small pile of granite rocks, lay a purple thistle on top to symbolize Stan's wisdom and his Scottish ancestry, and pour water from the Merced River to acknowledge its preciousness for life. I end by humming a bagpipe tune.

Since Stan had never been on top of El Cap, I point out the sights to him. We have a clear view of the top of Three Brothers next to us, Half Dome and Glacier Point across the valley, and dozens of snow-covered peaks like Red, Merced, Clark, and Starr King in the distance. My red-tailed hawk soars overhead, pay-ing its respects. More of my family is present as I'm wearing my grandfather's shirt, worn thin by his years and my years of hiking in it, my dad's durable olive-green army socks from the Korean War that don't ever seem to wear down, and the kind of lunch that Ev would have packed. For family and friends who will never see this view because of the hike's physical demands, I take pictures. Recounting the hike up, I realize that I crossed over six canyons, which would make El Cap the Seventh Mountain, a term that the ancient Chinese associated with the home of the gods. And it feels that way, sitting with this astounding view out over the Sierra Nevada with a pine-scented breeze flowing up from the valley.

I'm familiar enough with the valley's history to know that anywhere I look, someone or something has probably died. For instance, across the valley, going from right to left, Dan Osman, a BASE jumper died on the Leaning Tower in 1998 when he made a miscalculation with the length of his rope. An Indian maiden drowned in Bridalveil Fall. The lone Jeffery pine on Sentinel Dome, which held on for so long in the most recent drought, died. (Ansel Adams took a black-and-white photo of it in 1940.) During the drought of 1976–77, hikers carried buckets of water to the tree and staved off its death for a while. Then, for almost three decades, it stood there with its bare, twisted trunk and branches as an iconic reminder of endurance. One climber fell off Sentinel Rock and another was killed in a rockslide on Glacier Point. And I'm sure there were dozens more deaths over the years.

El Cap has its own litany of the dead. Besides the climbers who've died on the way up from hypothermia, equipment failures, or stone breaking off in their hands, others have successfully reached the top and stood up to congratulate each other, only to slip on loose gravel and fall to their deaths. Every day coyotes, hawks, and eagles kill birds, deer, squirrels, and rabbits. The peregrine falcon or goshawk that zipped through the trees a short while ago was probably hunting its prey. Under this amazing beauty there is ugliness. The Greeks felt that Persephone had another face when she was underground, not one of innocence but of terror for those who had crossed her. Can I see the beauty of nature knowing that what is here is because of what isn't here, because something else died? And yet, all the people who died here chose to come, and perhaps they didn't mind since their last days were spent in the valley.

The stories and mythologies of many cultures address common human struggles, fear of death, and the hidden geography of the mysteries that live within us. Little Red Riding Hood encounters monsters in the forest. Dante gets lost in his dark woods. Orpheus tries to save his wife, Eurydice, from the underworld to overcome his grief. Persephone is kidnapped and taken underground. Alice goes down the rabbit hole in Wonderland and falls into the anarchy of Greek gods updated to British royalty behaving badly. But more than explaining why life always seems to come with death attached, stories like these also involve journeys that start with the trauma life brings us. Some people journey through the underworld and come back, like Dante's trip down into Hell, through Purgatory, and up into Paradise with new insights into how to live. Some remain in the turmoil for the good of others, like Persephone's sacrifice so that crops would grow again and feed the people. A modern example of this is my friend Nicole, the organ transplant coordinator who willing endures the grief of a family who has just lost a loved one in order to help life come out of death. But some people get stuck in the tragedy, like Ahab, who was so focused on exacting revenge for his lost leg that he lived in a world of anger and retribution.

In the Akkadian myth, Inanna had to pass through seven gates to get into the underworld and had to give up something precious at each gate. At the end she had nothing left except herself, naked. This is how those who lose loved ones feel. And if I do not let go of my grief I will become Ahab. Today's hike has taken me up seven mountains. Have I arrived at a new place?

As I leave El Cap my senses are buzzing with sights and sounds. On the trail there is fresh bear scat, and I look closely to see what this bear has been eating. Only manzanita berries are identifiable. Having been mildly aware of wild animals on the way up—focused as I was on staying on the trail—I now react to every stick that snaps, every large shadow that flickers in the corner of my eye, every rock that tumbles down a slope for no apparent reason. I double-check my food to make sure it's sealed air tight and there are no cookie smells to attract animals with highly developed noses. Besides no other people around, now there are no birds chirping nor squirrels digging. What has scared them into silence? I go on alert.

An hour later I'm preoccupied with the ninety-degree heat and the persistent flies that want to use the moisture inside my nose as a sauna. A loud cry of pain erupts fifty yards ahead and I freeze. Two brown shapes rush into the brush. A small bear scoots up a tree while the larger animal stays hidden below. My first thought is that a mountain lion had the drop on a bear, but the fur color was off. This area is known to be home territory for one lion. I conclude that the second animal was the mother bear. The sound I heard might have been a yelp from the cub after being swatted by its mother for not moving fast enough. If it's a mountain lion, I'm supposed to stand tall and look big and intimidating. If it's a bear, the rangers say I should get down and look as small and as passive as possible. If it's a mother bear or lion, God help me.

I stay motionless for a long ten minutes, preparing for an attack, trying to be ready to drop to the ground, act big, or run, frantically trying to remember what I do for which. But no animal comes charging toward me. Since the only trail goes by that tree, I slowly make a wide detour to the right over granite rocks that shift and squeak under foot, hoping I don't disturb any rattlesnakes sunning themselves. As I move past the bears a hundred feet away, the cub looks around and climbs down. Over the next mile I frequently turn around to see if anything is sneaking up behind me, including the mountain lion that I have yet to see. Mile mark 14.

There are specific smells on this hike, and I can tell what terrain I'm walking through by sniffing—trees, flowers, bushes, open land, creeks. Occasionally I pick up a few stray scents. Before I saw the bears, I noticed a musky scent and wondered, "What is that?" And one specific smell told me that the climbers I met earlier did not make it to a conventional bathroom. I learn how animals can pick up human scents so easily, as well as the scents of peanut butter sandwiches and cookies, especially if I hold my mouth open a little and breathe in through both my mouth and nose. Animals simply know what their homes smell like.

Mid Afternoon—None. Back at the top of The Climb of Ten Thousand Steps, I begin the long and boring hike back down, thankful for making it to this point without getting attacked by lions, bears, or rattlesnakes. I'm so grateful for the deliciously cool shade after being in the hot sun for hours that I get distracted. When I start heading uphill, I realize that something is wrong and backtrack until I find the trail I want. At the junction with the Old Big Oak Flat Trail, at mile mark 17, I decide to go left instead of right. I haven't scouted this trail, but looking at my map I calculate there's enough time to make it back before dark since it will take me down to the foot of El Cap. I head left, excited about being spontaneous in the wilderness. Although there's little that I can see of the valley because of the thick forest cover, the old roadbed is wide with an easy, descending grade and a cool breeze. Leaves have accumulated on the surface to the depth of a couple of inches, making a soft cushion for my feet.

I'm gliding down the gentle decline, bouncing on the springiness of the leaves and whistling, enjoying my reward for a hard hike and expecting to saunter down to the valley floor.

Every time the road curves to the right to go around a bend, the crafted stonework that holds the old highway to the valley wall is evident. Now and then a clearing through the trees allows a view of the canyon wall on the other side and I measure my progress back into the valley. The fractures in the southern wall are exquisite and the afternoon light is highlighting every detail. I notice a scooped canyon by Stanford Point, the stain of a seasonal waterfall I've never seen between Stanford and Old Inspiration Point, and a parallel pillar to the right of Leaning Tower. Partway down, two off-white granite boulders the size of coffee tables sit in the middle of the road with lines a symmetrical four inches apart, looking like Chinese pottery that has a cracked, porcelain glaze. They seem out of place, as if they had fallen out of the back of a truck that was taking them to the Ahwahnee Hotel for an art display seventy years ago.

The trail leaves the cool shade beneath the trees and pushes through a thick stand of manzanita bushes when it reaches the Rockslides, the part of the valley wall that has crumbled away because of the close jointing of the rock. Mile mark 19. At Fireplace Bluffs I check Bridalveil Fall for rainbows but the flow of water is too light and wispy today to create any. To my despair and annoyance the trail also ends here. Frequent slides over the years have wiped out the remains of the road, which is why it was abandoned. This I knew. But a ranger assured me yesterday that there was still a hiking trail leading through. "Where!" I shout today, loud enough for him to hear, wherever he is, adding a few choice words. My lovely stroll is over.

Now it's too late in the day to retrace my steps and take the other trail. Resigning myself to whatever my fate will be, I follow a few stone ducks onto a gravel path. The ducks disappear and I lose track of the nebulous trail. I line a tree up on the other side of the Rockslides, some two hundred yards in the distance, and head for that, climbing over five-foot rocks in the hot sun. Detouring around knots of boulders that seem ready to untie and tumble, I lose sight of my tree, reorient, head off again, and reach a series of gullies that have gutted the middle of the boulder field.

Wiping sweat out of my eyes, I look down into the steep slide where everything is ready to roll downhill at the slightest touch but clings precariously to the sixty-degree slope. I take a deep breath and plunge down, hanging onto the branches of trees that have been uprooted by boulders bouncing down the canyon wall, slide twenty-five feet to the bottom of the sharply angled crevasse, then reverse the process by grabbing at tree roots in order to scramble and pull my way up the other side, all the while trying to keep my balance so that I don't go tumbling down the slope. I repeat this process at the second gully. And the next. The gullies are so steep that even boulders aren't able to find places to rest. Every time I slip, I slide a quick twenty feet down the slope and wonder if this entire shifting hillside is about to break loose in an avalanche. Every loose stone that turns under foot scoops out another cup of energy, and there isn't much left. Remembering that Muir once chewed artemesia leaves to keep his mind alert when he was in danger of falling off a narrow ledge, I scan the rocks for something to scrape off, stuff in my mouth, and eat.

I did not want to be doing this in bright afternoon sun after a long hike. It feels like 110 degrees on the heated rocks, and the sun is baking a glaze of color on the back walls of my eyes. I'm hot, sweaty, dehydrated, and probably experiencing a touch of sunstroke. When I close my eyes, I feel trail grit grinding under my lids. Far below, the cool, blue Merced River twinkles with ripples of cool air and I can hear people frolicking in the cool water, intentionally taunting me. I could pass out and simply die, all for the lack of a cup of cool water, my body desiccating on these hot rocks like the skin of a newt.

Finally I make it through the Rockslides but still there is no trail in sight. Hoping I'm above it, I begin bulling my way down the slope through the trees and bushes, stumbling and crashing, not caring in my dazed state what I'm trampling down or knocking over, until I find the trail sixty yards further down the valley wall. My eyes are glassy and even though I know I'm dehydrated, I can't make myself drink any more water. When I try, my body shakes. I'm so tired that my body flops along rather than strides. My mind has one focus, and one focus only: get to the end of this trail, quick. There is no enjoyment going on. No rest breaks or sightseeing. Any sprains or blisters that form now are on their own.

Thankfully, the middle part of the old road is in good condition because I just cannot take anything else. I make the big turn at the bend and El Capitan rises up in full majesty, glowing golden in the afternoon sun. Set against the deep blue of the sky, the sight takes my breath away. Realizing, even in my delirium, that I stood on top of it a few hours ago leaves me feeling incredibly insignificant. I try to shake off my walking stupor and stare hard at this image because I want to remember this. I'm now down to the level of Bridalveil Fall across the way, six hundred feet above the valley floor.

When I reach the valley floor, I can't feel my legs and sit flat on the ground, relieved that I didn't damage or break any major body parts. Mile mark 21. I desperately want to lie down in the grass and not move, and just stare blankly into the unseeing distance until the sun sets, I cool down, and feel a little better. But when the sun disappears I will be cold, hungry, and still an hour from camp. A coyote trots by, welcoming me back with a suspicious grin. What does it know that I don't? Trying to form a coherent thought is like digging in clay, but knowing that I can't lie down, I get up. After fourteen hours of hiking, already three more than I emotionally planned, I'm so tired that I can barely manage a smile for successfully taking on a challenge. Ninety minutes later, after trudging ever so slowly back on the road, I go to Degnan's, chug down thirty-two ounces of cold energy drink, and don't feel the need for a bathroom. Mile mark 24.

Pulling myself onto a shuttle to take me back to camp, because I don't ever want to walk again, I'm irritated to the point of yelling at the people on the bus who are oblivious to the glorious revelations on display everywhere around them and who don't seem to care that I almost died. They are preoccupied with where to eat, whether they should get off the bus here or a spot further down the road, and by a child tossing a rock that he seems incapable of catching, repeatedly dropping it on the floor of the bus with a thunk. Thunk. Thunk. I want to throw the kid and his rocks out the window. I'm back to reality. Whoopee.

Twilight—Vespers. I need to be quiet now if I'm going to reclaim the peace I found on the first part of the hike. I take my first shower in four days and feel a little better, free of the caked mixture of trail dust and sweat. Back in camp, my simple dinner plans are upset by new arrivals from France who've taken over the table as they prepare a three-course meal complete with wine glasses. It's nice. It's elegant. Camp 4 rarely sees anything as elaborate as this. But I'm in no mood for it. I storm back to Degnan's and scarf a big bag of chips and a liter of cold soda, wanting to celebrate the hike somehow even though this doesn't make me feel any better, just distracted. I still don't have to go to the bathroom and I'm beginning to realize how dangerously dehydrated I was.

Last Hour—Compline. I let go of my frustration and walk sluggishly to the river where water from the meditative pool at the bottom of Yosemite Falls enters the meadow. I watch the last of the sunset paint the valley walls golden orange. My body still radiates heat from the hike, so I sink my abused feet into the dark, tranquil river to cool down. Pouring water over my arms with cupped hands, each movement becoming more painful as stiffness settles in, I read the evening devotion from the prayer book of the Monastery of Mart Maryam in South India: "Glory to you, creator of the days and nights, who have wakened us to praise you." Those monks knew something about human suffering, about enduring oppressive heat, about accepting death as an affirmation of the preciousness of life. I imagine they have a prayer for times when the sun has baked your brains, you've encountered wild animals, and flies have feasted on your sweat.

Nature has humbled me today and taught me a lesson. Death does not interrupt life, life interrupts death. Only by taking risks do I stay alive.

Breaking Open to Falling Leaves

Everything alike drenched in gold light, heaven's colors
coming down to the meadows and groves, making every leaf
a romance, air, earth, and water in peace beyond thought.

—John Muir, *Our National Parks*

When I wasn't looking, everything changed. After living above
the north side of Yosemite all summer, the sun shifts south to
rise, travel, and set directly over the east-west axis of the valley,
highlighting thousands of granite features on the vertical walls
that before now were overlooked. The hot, steamy weather of
August has been replaced by warm days and cool nights. Mornings are brisk in the meadows once again. The sky turns cobalt
blue but everything green is beginning to brighten with yellow.
The infrequent rain has left dust to settle and cover the leaves of
the trees and bushes in a diaphanous layer of gray gauze. Fewer
people come to the valley in September, uncluttering the trails
for meandering walks and thoughts of what has been.

As light begins to rise over the mountains, I eat a simple breakfast of granola at a table in the lingering darkness of Camp 4. I
hear a low "bong" every three seconds that sounds as if one of

the Japanese climbers is tapping a hollow metal object with a wooden mallet as part of some morning Buddhist rite. My friend Molly thinks it's a flammulated owl, a small creature that eats insects and has flame-like coloration on its feathers. I wish there were more light so that I could get a glimpse.

After breakfast and morning coffee, Bob and Suzy, Liz and Tom begin organizing their climbing equipment in my campsite. They're from Southern California and are traveling around together. Their fingers are strained and taped together for support, some with cracked fingertips that are black with bruises, and scrapes mar the backs of their hands. With reverence they spread blue tarps on the ground and smooth the creases. They lay out the different kinds of climbing gear they'll need and organize it by function—carabiners, tapers, hexentrics, tri-cams, and other kinds of chocks to stick into cracks, pitons and bolts used to provide some measure of safety; belay devices and harnesses, sixty-meter nylon ropes; duct tape to repair everything, including ripped pants; water bottles and two days of food. All the items are packed carefully into the four-foot-tall canvas climbing bags as if they were the Eucharist. Wounded hands will distribute these elements; they will help heal and strengthen the climbers' spirits. The couples shoulder their 150-pound bags of gear and head out to climb a route on Sentinel Rock. On the north side of camp Horst, a German climber from Bremen, plays songs from the Andes Mountains on his wooden flute. Beautiful and haunting in a way that unsettles me.

Tuolumne Meadows

I head for Tuolumne Meadows. On the way up I drive by the side of massive domes and mutter in exasperation, "These are the scenes I spend hours hiking to, and here they are along the road!" I console myself with the thought that much of the importance of a journey of discovery is the journey itself, not the destination, because it's along the way that one interacts with the natural world and learns from it. Tuolumne Meadows is at an elevation of 8,600 feet in the high Sierra. Two miles long, it's already in full autumn colors after a summer that lasted barely one month. I get out of the car and wander though the meadow, breathing the crisp forty-five-degree air. The clear high-altitude sky radiates a deep blue that shimmers off the narrow stream winding through. The meadow feels like it's the center of the world and everything else is revolving around it. There are only a few trees here and no canyon walls to block my view of the light granite domes and peaks of the Sierra crest that encircle us, all dusted with the white of new snow.

A coyote's howl shatters the midday peace. I finally spot his ears sticking above the brown meadow grass a hundred feet away. I thought coyotes only howled at night. Maybe he's protecting his territory and telling me to stay away. Maybe he's sharing his midday joy. Or perhaps he's calling for his mate who's died, a sorrow he will mourn until his own death. I move quietly away.

On the north side of the meadow I find Soda Springs, with its fabled carbonated drinking water still bubbling up from the ground as well as Parson's Cabin, designed by Bernard Maybeck, the architect of many of the wooden Arts and Crafts homes built in Berkeley during the late 1800s. The cabin was built for the Sierra Club when it was founded by John Muir and others. It was the starting point for their outings into the backcountry, and it's still in use today. I ask a ranger riding by on horseback if it's possible to hike up nearby Cathedral Peak, Muir's favorite in the park. He says it's good hiking most of the way, then the peak goes into class 4 or 5 mountain climbing. I doubt that Muir used any ropes when he went to the top; he was simply agile, determined, and a little foolhardy. Ev would worry that now I'd want to hike up the peak. And I do, reasoning that if Muir could make it up without killing himself, I could, too, being similarly determined and sometimes stupid about these things. But I don't have enough time today and will have to come back. Although Unicorn Peak, the one to the left of Cathedral that looks like a three-sided pyramid, is similar in height to Cathedral, the ranger thinks it's only class 3 and can be hiked to the top. Falls from there, he says, are not always fatal.

Leaving the meadow, I enter the forest and follow a trail under the trees that eventually emerges into the open along the Lyell Fork of the Tuolumne River. The river channel is a gallery of tan rock sculptures and water flowing around and through what the river has patiently carved. The water is so close to the skin of the sky that it seems to pulse with its heartbeat, and its cascades twinkle in the bright afternoon sun with the eyes of the Ahwahnechees' Great Spirit. I lie down and listen as the water flows around the sculptures. As the breeze flows over my skin, I fall asleep and imagine the Great Spirit entering and inspiring me with visions of what can be, now that my future has been taken away.

I leave the river by looping back to the meadows where my hike started, then see two Mountain bluebirds whose color is so intense that it seems the sky has soaked into their feathers. Emotionally I'm not ready to leave this stunning scenery, so I tack on a hike to the top of Lembert Dome. Parts of the steep three-mile trail are washed out, forcing me to scramble on all fours to get around the small rockslides on the mountain slope. Once on top I look over the length of the meadows clothed in their red and yellow autumn colors, at the blue granite peaks on the horizon, and at the black ominous ones in the distance that

I saw in July near Tioga Pass, which seemed to clench death in its canyons. The wind is strong because this is the highest point in the area and no mountains are in the way to slow it down. I zip my jacket and batten my hat to keep it on. I'm standing in the sky at 9,400 feet, trying to be careful with my footing so the wind doesn't blow me off.

On the way back to the valley I stop at Tenaya Lake. The water reflects the deep azure of the sky but the main colors of this landscape are gray granite, white snow, and a few patches of dark green where scraggy pine trees were able to root themselves in the small pockets of soil that accumulated in the crevices of the mountains. It's a barren, exposed environment. Eadweard Muybridge, Ansel Adams, and Edward Weston all took photographs of the lake; some of their photos were moody while others were elegant and sublime. Today the sun is warm on my skin but the breeze is cool due both to the altitude and its having swept over the snow on the way here. It feels like the week I spent one summer canoeing in the Boundary Waters of Canada, where the air never warmed up enough to take off my coat.

In the valley I have only enough energy left to sit like a plant, so I head for a meadow, plop down, and vegetate. There aren't many flowers left—some white peregrine thistles, goldenrod, a six-foot stand of woolly mullein, which always make me think of hairy dinosaurs, and a few Yosemite asters. I watch a family of acorn woodpeckers, costumed in their clownish white, black, and red outfits, fly repeatedly across Cook's Meadow with hundreds of acorns and then push them into holes they had drilled out earlier in dead trees. I'm content to watch them work. After an hour I move over to the river and sit near the bulrushes, fascinated by the movement of one peculiar insect that hovers over the surface of the water before touching down, apparently to feed, then it's back in the air before touching down again. Up and down, up and down, each time a foot away from the previous spot and in a perfectly straight line.

Clouds Rest Hike

As dawn paints a pink line on the dark horizon, I begin a twenty-three-mile hike, crossing the meadows to the east end of the valley where the trail begins. In September it's as far as I can go and still get back before darkness returns. The journey consists of five hours of steady uphill climbing to reach Clouds Rest, a meal break on top, then five hours hiking back down. Clouds Rest is the highest point visible from the valley floor. Rising to ten thousand feet, the peak received its name because clouds passing by often seemed to get caught on its rocks. Unlike most of my hikes, there are no alternating segments of uphill and downhill hiking that will give each set of leg muscles a chance to rest. I will wear them both out, like grinding a stick shift up the Berkeley hills then riding the brakes back down them. The only relief is in the flat area on the trail above Nevada Fall that goes by the entrance to Little Yosemite Valley, and even that section has a moderate uphill grade. Today's hike is two hours longer than the hike up Half Dome and goes a thousand feet higher in elevation.

WATERFALLS

Yosemite National Park is an oval of 1,170 square miles; most of it is designated as wilderness. There are 800 miles of hiking trails. The Valley is seven miles long and one mile wide at its widest point. Many waterfalls are seasonal and dependent upon rain, and Yosemite Falls can be dry by August. Some falls like Vernal, Nevada, Illilouette, and

Bridalveil flow all year round because their source of water
is snow melting in the highlands.

Yosemite	2,425 ft.
Sentinel	2,000 ft.
Ribbon	1,612 ft.
Staircase	1,300 ft.
Bridalveil	620 ft.
Nevada	594 ft.
Vernal	317 ft.

Because I've been here so often, I've begun to take the enormous
size of everything for granted. For example, Bridalveil now seems
like a quaint, little waterfall and Yosemite a normal-sized one,
until I realize that Yosemite is twice the height of the Empire
State Building and Bridalveil is as tall as the arch in St. Louis.
Sentinel Falls, second in height in the valley, is two hundred feet
taller than the CN Tower in Toronto, which once was the world's
tallest building. Even thick, muscular Vernal Fall, the shortest
in the valley and looking rather stubby at 317 feet, approaches
twice the height of the Leaning Tower of Pisa.

Quickly I move past both Vernal and Nevada Falls. Unlike
the trail to Half Dome that was mostly under tree cover, there
are plenty of sights along this trail to take my mind off the unre-
lenting uphill grind. The view south over the Sierra range shows
pockets of snow clinging to the north side of mountains. Snow
fell there last weekend, hinting at the winter already returning
to the highlands, but some of the snow never melted from previous winters. The shadow sides of these peaks also contain the
residual glaciers that John Muir staked with wooden markers to
map their movements 140 years ago. Mount Clark's flank shows

a dark spot that must be a thousand feet in diameter. Clark is an odd-shaped peak, anyway, looking like a fin sticking up in the air, so it might as well have a hole in it, too. I watch the spot as I hike along to see if it moves and I can determine if it's the shadow of a passing cloud or something else, but nothing changes. It's probably a major depression left after a circle of granite the size of a city block broke off, and the sun is hitting it just right.

Starting up the left side of Clouds Rest as it emerges from under the thinning forest and rises above the tree line, I turn around. I've never been high enough to look down on Half Dome before and the trail is still climbing higher. Half Dome's face no longer looks flat. In fact, the whole complex appears as supporting shoulders below a face that looks as though an ice cream scoop has taken part of the mountain away, not a dome that was neatly sliced in half like a loaf of bread, which is how it looks from the valley floor. From Glacier Point, Half Dome looks like the side of a thumb sticking up. Below the face is a big chest of rubble that climbers have to scramble up before they begin to climb.

On this left side of Clouds Rest, on the smooth ridge that rises to the peak, two large, stony knobs stick out. From the valley these protuberances look tiny, but one of them has the dimensions of a small sailing ship, the *Niña* or the *Pinta* on another journey to a new land. The second knob is smaller and looks like a stack of weathered, layered rock that one would see at Wisconsin Dells. Indian Arch, on the other side of this canyon, has the same layered look. I finish one bottle of water and close it, having learned my lesson about dehydration on the El Capitan hike when I suffered from heat stroke. Today I keep a bottle in my hand and drink even when I'm not thirsty. On a long hike like this, my backpack will weigh twenty pounds, most of it water.

Although it's my first time on Clouds Rest, I feel as though I'm

hiking with the mountain on a journey to see what we can discover together today. No other human beings are around. Puffing
up the last steep bit of trail toward the ten-thousand-foot mark,
my heart is beating around two hundred times a minute and it
doesn't calm even though I'm resting as much as I'm walking. I
trudge fifty feet then rest, fifty feet then more rest, breathing hard
and thinking that it's heart attack time. It's frustrating having to
slow down this close to the top but I'd like to be conscious when
I get there. Hiking two miles into the sky is more difficult than I
thought. Living near the coast at an elevation of thirty-four feet
probably has something to do with it.

Finally, I'm standing on top of Clouds Rest and the world
falls away at my feet, feeling like the wanderer in Caspar David
Friedrich's painting, who stands on a mountain peak above the
clouds. The blue of Tenaya Lake sparkles to the north. Olmsted Point is visible closer in but is rather unimpressive as I look
down on it from this height. Half Dome looks like a child's toy.
Across Tenaya Canyon, Mount Watkins's flank is almost as sheer
as Clouds Rest's. There is no wind at all on the peak, which is
surprising, and the air is so light that it doesn't hold the heat and
I have to put a jacket on even though it's eighty degrees in the
valley. The pinnacle itself is about five feet wide and forty feet
long with severe drop-offs on all sides, but there's enough space
to lie down and recover from the hike up. By comparison, the
tops of the domes I've been on—North, Sentinel, and Half—are
all wide open and nicely rounded. The top of El Capitan is huge
but steeply slanted. Eagle Peak is just a point.

Walking to the edge, I look straight down the side of Clouds
Rest and see six thousand feet of slick granite polished by the
glaciers and shining like stainless steel. It doesn't feel scary. The
dead drop from Glacier Point of thirty-five hundred feet unsettles

me more than this, and Glacier has a railing to hold me back if I lose my footing on the gravelly rock. The view down seems like one wild, out-of-control toboggan ride rather than anything dangerous, although the stop would be abrupt because of the tree trunks at the bottom.

I stare at the forest below and try to locate my grotto of ferns that has two thirty-foot-tall waterfalls, even tracing the river as it flows down Tenaya Canyon into the forest, but I do not find it. Though it doesn't take great nerve to stand there with my toes hanging over the side so I'm able to take a photograph—losing sight of the edge as I look through the view finder—it does take something else to compose a second picture after realizing what a mere puff of wind would do to my precarious balance. I back away.

Leaving the pinnacle, a yellow-bellied marmot catches sight of me and slips over the edge up ahead. I hurry down and watch what looks like a woodchuck, or a really fat squirrel, pause on the next level as it monitors my movements. It goes down another level and waits for me to catch up. Behind Clouds Rest, twenty blackbirds soar through the sky in circles that go up and down as if they were in a velodrome. I didn't know that blackbirds could fly at this altitude. Half an hour down the trail, new bear and deer tracks appear, but no fresh scat. Like me, they're just passing through.

At the junction with the trail to Half Dome I finally see another person, and we share our stories as we hike down. Jack is from the midlands of England, a retired engineer and a biker. He said his hardest ride was a cycling race up the Sierra Nevada in Spain that went to an altitude of eighty-five hundred feet. During the race he timed his heart rate at 180, so he hasn't minded the climbing on this trail. Because of cycling, his thighs are doing fine. Mine keep shaking after I convince Jack that we should stop and rest. Back on the flat valley floor, I slip into Degnan's, order an Italian sub from Diane, and gulp down a large bottle of energy drink. I drank eighty ounces of water on the trail, which may seem like a lot, but the continual exercise over the course of the hike makes it average out to only one cup an hour. I pull out the empty water bottle I closed on top of Clouds Rest to refill it and find it compressed in half by the change in altitude. Thankfully my lungs are doing fine.

The sign outside the ranger station says there will be a lunar eclipse tonight over Half Dome, so at dusk I head for Cook's Meadow. As I assemble my camera equipment, people gather around. They think I know where the moon will rise because I have a tripod. Stylishly dressed people come out into the twilight from the bright lights of the lodge. A few are clad in plaid and pastel wear, walking slowly and carefully, not used to the dark or the uneven ground. Some carry glasses of wine they didn't finish at dinner, as well as blankets to sit on. Climbers from Camp 4 wander out in torn pants and dusty shirts, and then lie down in the grass.

The wild animals and birds of the meadow notice the invasion taking place and excuse themselves, retreating to the boulders and trees under the cliffs. Silhouetted along the rim of the valley, four thousand feet away, trees stand stiff as sentinels guarding the valley and hold the last yellow, orange, and red of the sunset—pines mostly, but also one grand old oak that has watched the movements of the sun and moon for more than a century.

As we wait we talk to each other about where the moon will rise. Seeing nothing at 7:16 p.m., the predicted time of the eclipse, we talk about when it might happen. After ten minutes of not seeing anything move, we lie back on the grass, smell the western violets and yarrow, and, like neighborhood kids, watch the stars twinkle in the night sky, and think of our parents and grandparents leaning back on warm September nights like this decades ago.

Meteors shoot overhead and burn out. Three satellites zip up from the horizon and fly at incredible speeds across the sky, reflecting the absent sun in bright points of light. One satellite could be the space station; someone thinks it's in the area. Airplanes with blinking, colored lights lumber along. In comparison to the satellites, the planes barely seem to be going fast enough to stay in the air. While the satellites make it across the entire sky in thirty seconds, the airplanes take so long that I forget and take them for new planes before realizing my mistake.

Tiny lights flicker on Half Dome's face and our conversation switches to the climbers "bedding down," crawling into hammocks hanging on pegs stuck into cracks in the vertical wall of rock. Some of us lying on solid ground think it would be cool to be with them, suspended in the dark air with three thousand feet of empty space below our legs, looking down on tiny people walking around the valley floor with flashlights. Others drone on and on about how hard it would be for them to fall asleep up there with no floor beneath their beds. What if the support peg pulled loose? How would they turn over? Do animals live in those walls? "Mice do," the climbers among us say, "and they steal shiny objects and your food." It feels good to hang out in the meadow like this, tacked to the side of a planet spinning around at enormous speeds and not being flung into space, chatting with strangers from around the world and feeling the bonds of the human community strengthening.

After ten more anxious minutes we finally see a glimmer of brightness just above Half Dome's right shoulder and a hush settles over us. The breeze stops blowing and the trees go still as if the event is about to begin. That, or an earthquake is getting ready to shake the valley, a shifting in the earth that only the trees and animals sense.

In John Muir's day a massive earthquake did hit Yosemite at 2:30 a.m. and shook the sturdy trees in the meadows so violently that many of their trunks snapped. Whole sections of granite walls broke off and cascaded into the meadows, waves of rock that flowed down in the moonlight and sent large boulders tumbling across the valley floor. Muir survived by ducking behind the trunk of a large ponderosa pine to protect himself from the boulders bouncing past, but strong aftershocks rumbled through the mountains for days, unnerving some people so much that they left for San Francisco on the first stagecoach out.

Personally, I'd like an earthquake to rumble through the lodge and take out the television sets, leaving people with nothing to do but talk to each other about what they had seen, what had stuttered them with awe, what had left them mute with feelings of grace. I'd like everyone to get out of climate-controlled rooms and sleep outdoors, get close to nature, which is why I think we came here. I'd like the earthquake to cut off the electric lights so that we could see how dark the night really is, how beautiful the stars, and how close we live among them.

Tonight we hold our breath and wait for the rest of the curtain to rise on the moon. I think some of us came to the eclipse hoping to feel the fear and terror that our distant ancestors may have felt when they watched something like this unfold in the heavens, unaware of the science behind it. Or when prophets and preachers predicted the arrival of the End not knowing what in their world was being destroyed, what was coming unglued from the pages of history, or what had chipped off the solid rock of time. Two hundred of us came into the meadow wanting to sound the depths of our own despair and touch whatever residual fears had been tucked into back pockets by our grandparents, although most of us would not speak of our unease in this way.

In the facing of our fears we touch something deeper, something basic to what it means to be human. No matter how much we try to convince ourselves we are in control of our lives, much of what we've built up as security is still at the mercy of nature: hurricanes, earthquakes, drought, floods, and blizzards.

In a way we came into the meadow to die, if that was to be our fate, to meet our end bravely. We would not hide from this. We would strengthen our resolve and together face this peril, this cold premonition of an ancient god that wants to take our light away, this massive cosmic monster hunting down our planet to devour.

Perhaps those of us who know astrophysics fear that the moon's absence means the twisted bundles of the earth's geomagnetic field and the solar winds that protect life on earth from the deadly stream of cosmic radiation have somehow failed. The moon is silently being pulled into the far side of the earth, and we were about to die a painful, prickly death. No matter. We would stand up like brave people of every generation have always stood up: fearful of what was happening but knowing that we must stand together, we must face this challenge, and we must speak of the glory that we've seen in the valley. And we would die.

Or not. It was only an eclipse, after all, an event more prone to our fantasies of destruction than the source of any real dread. Some of the people staying in the lodge even brought baguettes and brie into the meadow for the seven o'clock show, while the climbers had hurried out from their campfires of hamburger, potatoes, and beans. We knew it wasn't going to be the death of all we held dear yet we came into the middle of the valley to be with others, to be reminded that we belong not just to the earth but to a solar system whose shiny planets ricochet through space like billiard balls on a black pool table and we belong to each other.

We came to stand in a meadow glowing with the last fire of sunset and entertain the fantasy of the cosmos breaking into billions and billions of shimmering pieces so that we could say we had experienced the fear that our ancestors felt. Some of us, I think, want to make sure that the moon really does return.

At this point anything could happen. Something is obviously wrong because there is no moon in front of us as the park rangers promised there would be, and they should know. Every day they post the exact times for sunrise and sunset.

Then a gust of wind rushes past, raising the hairs on our arms, and we ready ourselves for some mighty force to surge over the Sierra Nevada and knock us off our feet, like Muir's storm that swept over a valley in Utah in a "torrent of wind thick with sand and dust." The moon rises but it's already in full eclipse, and rather than being a demonically inflamed red circle, a planet glowing as a burning cinder or extinguished black by the earth's dark shadow, the moon is smoky. Collectively we sigh with disappointment, releasing the tense air we've been holding in. When we realize that this gray disk is as good as the view's going to get, people drift back to their cabin lights and campsites. I stay and chat with a few others.

Nature has let us down. We're finally away from the city lights and we've actually taken the time to step away from our televisions and iPods to watch an entire eclipse that should be spectacular. It isn't. Yet a sense of community has formed because we left our places of comfort and faced the unknown together. People who would not normally talk to each other because of how they were dressed did talk, asking why they had come to Yosemite—and our casual questions opened the doors to deeper conversations.

After half an hour, a bright dot appears on the moon's left edge that slowly expands into a slender crescent. The moon gradually turns white and blinds us from the fainter light of the stars we had been enjoying in the moon's absence. Some of these stars exist only in the light now reaching us, the stars themselves having burned out long ago or gone supernova, like Cassiopeia A with its tie-dyed colors of green, blue, red, and yellow. The rest of the people leave.

Now alone in the meadow, I continue to wait as the brightness of the moon illuminates the valley, longing for the darkness of deep night to return with the stars' last, sweet eulogies of light.

By morning the trickle of water in Yosemite Falls, which has been stoutly hanging on in the months without rain, stops, leaving a long, moist ribbon of green moss where the falls used to be. Under the trees, squirrels pull handfuls of dry pine needles back and peer underneath to see if there are any acorns to eat. I walk down to the Royal Arches and chat with a mother who is calmly knitting while her sons climb above, trusting them not to take any unnecessary risks. I continue on to Mirror Meadow, stepping down to the sand of the old lake bed where a meadow is forming, remembering when the lake's still reflections of Half Dome and Mount Watkins had brought that stillness within me. I don't stay long, feeling anxious about something that has been with me this entire trip.

Today Indian Summer comes and fills the valley with air that is the temperature of mindlessness—neither warm nor cool enough to notice—of a degree that is slightly refreshing. The day is well suited for wandering from place to place without destination or purpose. I relax into it and wear it like skin.

I saunter six miles down toward the west end of the valley, stopping to examine the animal tracks on the trail, trying to figure out whose territory I'm hiking through. There are various kinds of shoe prints, including some with stiletto heels. These may be walking stick marks. I identify the coyote prints, which look like dog tracks, then the squirrel marks, which have a short main pad and pointy pads for each finger and toe, and then deer tracks that look like the side prints of two thumbs. Now the intriguing marks appear. Raccoons have made the small hand-like tracks, but I doubt there are any three- toed sloths, even though one set looks like that. A few marks are bear tracks, claws on the end of wide human footprints, but I don't see any large catlike tracks that were made by mountain lions. Yet there are a few partial prints I can't identify.

Leaving the trail, I enter the unknown forest down by Cathedral Rocks, a little worried that bears might live here and take exception to being disturbed. People don't come into this forest in the west end of the valley, and after half an hour of walking in it I realize why. The thick forest of trees hides the great views of the valley walls that I could see from above on the northside trail that winds through the Rockslides, the river is somewhere else, and the woods are absent of sound rather than quiet.

Sitting on a fallen branch in this blank solitude of place, I wait. Perhaps the Ahwahnechees' god of creation will walk by, trailing a robe of mist and stars that I keep looking for. Maybe a mountain lion will show up for a moment in the spot of sunlight atop the moraine of land left by the last retreating glacier, before it slides back into the woods. Perhaps a hiker will come along the trail, having lost the way, and we'll have a great conversation. But after an hour of waiting for something that never comes, I conclude there's nothing here except these rather ordinary trees. There's no edge between forest and meadow where owls, coyotes, and mice congregate, because there's no meadow. Even the sky is blocked from view. There are no sounds except for a few birds and squirrels, and even they seem lost in these woods.

I try to shake my unsettledness by searching for the river by using my keen wilderness skills, honed by months of hiking and camping, to divine the flow of the land. Maybe taking a blind step toward something will encourage that something to move closer toward me. After fumbling fruitlessly in different directions, I find the river by walking in a straight line across the valley's width. The receding water of autumn has left isolated pools in the gravel bed along the sides of the river that continues to surge past on its way out of the mountains and on to the great Central Valley.

The stillness of the pools and the astounding scenery I've seen this week tell me that each season has its own special beauty that ends when the season is over, giving way to the beauty of the next. Human life has its seasons, too, as much as I rebel against death. Yet I know that every day animals die in Yosemite, and every day climbers take risks and some of them die. But death in nature is accepted when it comes, even when it seems to come too early, as when fawns die. And I was reminded while waiting with others for the lunar eclipse that each of us is part of something larger, the human community, and this continues after each of us is gone. That Evelyn died is not a tragedy to the world, yet it has been hard for me to accept. But it has happened, whether I accept it or not. Emotionally I feel myself turning like the seasons, trying to make the transition from the goodness that had been our life together to the unknown of what will be, trying to believe that it's okay to let go. The blooming of life with Evelyn is over, and I need to turn fallow.

These common trees, the warm air, and the still water become my elements of communion. I listen to the rich silence of the forest. In these simple, pleasant woods there is enough to feed my heart. Here the world's veil is pulled back for me to see clearly. Here the world is cracked apart for healing and rest, broken open so that life will continue to flow like a river and be consumed, that it might nourish. The old tectonic plates shift and new life rises with mountains and rivers and birds that like to dance in the water.

The soft slide of autumn's breeze through the valley's trees shifts the angle of millions of leaves on the aspen trees that line the river to the north, toward the approaching cold season of winter when trails will freeze as hard as stone and snow will cover the mountains under a thick blanket of white. Today the leaves shimmer in the warm hours of the afternoon, hypnotically drawing me further in. Ev's absence becomes a reassuring presence as I realize that I can carry her memories within me. My patient waiting becomes an entrance, and I feel excitement for the first time in months. Dr. Seuss said: "Don't cry because it's over. Smile because it happened."

Leaves of oak and dogwood release, fall, twirl onto the path, and curl around on the surface of the meandering stream until they catch the edge of an eddy that slightly, then slowly, swirls them behind a crest of rocks that rise like a miniature range of mountains above the surface of the river. I break under this beauty and let go of the past that I might begin my new journey. Pieces of my heart pull away with the movement of the leaves, filter down through the water, and paper the pebbled bottom of the pool with splashes of red, yellow, and brown. Water mites send concentric circles out across the surface of the still water as they skitter on hair-thin feet. Moss in the rocks on shore slumber in the nestled heat of the afternoon sun. The hope that I'd forgotten under sorrow finds a place to open its battered hands in the middle of this valley, in a quiet woods surrounded by white granite mountains that float through the lazy autumn river of space.

Unmarked Trails

Everybody needs beauty as well as bread ... where Nature
may heal and cheer and give strength to body and soul alike.

—John Muir, *The Yosemite*

"Who?" he asks. I open one eye and watch someone stumble
through the dark. "Who?" he asks again. Confused, I can't remember where I am or why the bed is so hard. Waking up, I'm
in Yosemite and an owl has been asking its own questions of
night's mysteries. Other campers rise and begin cooking breakfast,
the blue flames of their gas stoves whooshing into the cold air
and lighting the black spaces between the fir trees. Overnight
temperatures slipped to the low forties, delaying movement in
Camp 4 as people savor the warmth of their sleeping bags. I
slide out of my bag, pour granola into a cup, add water, and go
on a morning walk.

In the woods by Rixon's Pinnacle thousands of ladybugs have
huddled into a red ball on the end of an uprooted tree to keep
warm. In Leidig Meadow a doe and her fawn are eating in the
same corner they occupied last night; the circle of matted grass
where they slept is off to the left. On the eastern horizon scal-

loped clouds turn bright orange as the hidden sun outlines the Sierra's jagged crest. When the sun climbs over the backside of Half Dome, its rays illuminate the red leaves of oak trees in front of the blue granite of the Royal Arches. The only plants still blooming in the meadows are rosy buckwheat, blue curls, and turkey mullein, a silvery-green plant with tiny light flowers and wide hairy leaves. Along the riverbank, spotted sandpipers walk along, poking at the beach, and a few dragonflies hover over the water. Volunteers at the chapel stretch and ready themselves to restore another part of the meadow. A new day begins.

Although the days in October cling to the warmth of summer, night's sharpness signals that the darkness increasingly belongs to winter. The rains have returned and released into the air the rich smells of fall. Autumn leaves drop from branches like weary travelers home after a long trip, opening up the sky and letting more of the high country's light flow down into the meadows. As the sun arcs lower through the Southern Hemisphere, the valley's plants shift from lingering green to glimmering gold and brown.

Four deer walk slowly across the Merced River into Cook's Meadow, the last one acting as a sentinel until the others are on the far bank. Then she starts over, pauses to drink, and catches up when the others find something to eat. I sit nearby and wait. Today I'm going to follow them and see where they hide during the middle part of the day. The deer settle down for a while under the oak trees, eat a few acorns, and move on, migrating from place to place for reasons that are unclear.

Now and then they bound off, spooked by something I don't hear, and leave little puffs of dust their feet kick up. Sometimes their wandering takes them across a stream but by the time I find a bridge and make it to the other side, I have to track them down again. Once I walked by, not spotting anything until I gave up and started for home. Then I saw big eyes blinking behind the bushes. Their tan fur matched the color of the dry grass. I lose them again while watching climbers make their way up the Royal Arches. When I look back down they're gone. Climbing over the ridge of rocks that line the trail and channel hikers elsewhere, I enter an unusually quiet woods. No trails are here. Animals have a sanctuary of their own from the eyes and chatter of people. I look for the deer only a little distance in before feeling that I'm intruding and decide to back out.

Over by Swinging Bridge, I sit on the riverbank and watch Sentinel Meadow for a few hours, getting a feel for the spot: discovering which plants grow here, which animals and birds come by, and which views of the valley can be seen as clouds flow over Eagle Peak and Yosemite Falls. I imagine pioneer children playing on the sandy beach and Native Americans a thousand years before that pulling rushes from the river to make baskets or soaking acorns in the water to leach out the bitterness. A squirrel trots by with its cheeks puffed out, stuffed full of leaves for its winter nest. It stops and somehow manages to push a stick into the mess, then continues on. Bucks of various ages get into contests of antler pushing in the meadow. It doesn't seem to be a challenge for dominance but rather a training session for the younger males on how to do it properly, like linemen drills for high school football players. My reverie is disrupted by two jays having a heated argument behind me. A third jay flies up, the two get things settled between them, and all is quiet again.

On this trip I entered using the lower route, driving through Gustine and Mariposa. In the area around the Kesterson Wildlife Refuge a thick tule fog slowed me down so much that I put on a CD of Celtic music and suddenly it seemed like I was driving across the Scottish moors. The problems of home and work slid

off as the music brought me into the present, with excitement
building over what discoveries this trip might hold. I followed
the course of the Merced River up the canyon to El Portal, past
the dilapidated buildings and abandoned shafts of gold and silver
mines that pocket the scraggy hills. The lust for precious metal
brought the miners into this area in the 1850s and into conflict
with the Ahwahnechees already living here.

Around noon I return to camp and meet new arrivals. We fall into
easy conversation and decide to combine efforts for lunch. Matt,
from Kentucky, fries up chicken and yams. Steve, from Oregon,
heats up green beans. I contribute chili, which seems a better option than peanut butter, my only other food in shareable quantity.
Steve is a computer programmer and began climbing in junior
high because it gave him a change of pace. Matt is an electrical
engineer and started climbing when he was twenty-three, figuring
it was better than hanging out in bars getting drunk. He likes to
attempt things he doesn't know if he can do. "El Capitan would
be a nice challenge," he says, "but there are too many people on
it." They'll try Washington Column first, the two-thousand-foot
column to the right of the Royal Arches.

This is the season when wildlife fattens up for winter. Bees
jump from one last fading flower to the next being as busy as,
well, bees. Female bears roam around, eating everything they
can find, battling chipmunks for nuts and hikers for backpacks,
all to satisfy the need to put on four inches of fat before winter
so embryos can take root and cubs will be born in the spring.
Steller's jays, red-shafted flickers, and robins chirp in the trees,
gray squirrels are burying acorns. The echoes of woodpeckers

systematically pounding nuts into holes can be heard around the valley as they rush to stock provisions before the squirrels and deer get them all.

Under the trees by Degnan's, I dodge the fattest acorns I've ever seen so they don't bruise my head. These acorns are striped, like watermelons. Others are long and lean. The acorns seen by Muir's bench are round and brown. By Sentinel Rock they are blue, and along the trail behind North Dome by Snow Creek the acorns are held in yellow cups. Could there be seven kinds of oak trees here to match the seven kinds of manzanita and seven strains of warblers, each having adjusted to a different environment? I sit with my coffee, thinking about the synchronicity of this and enjoying the warm touch of the afternoon sun in the cool breeze. I open a book and let the words of Muir, Clark, and Bunnell fatten me up with enough stories to last the winter.

I head off hiking around the valley to see what history I can discover, wanting to explore the places that I normally rush by on my way to long hikes. At the Indian Caves, two butterflies—a black and yellow swallowtail and a California Sister with orange, black, and white colors—flutter around a stand of violet wandering daisies. The pair's shadow dances on the dark granite wall behind them like Thai puppets depicting the transitory nature of life—for butterflies, flowers, and the warmth of this day.

It's unclear which caves the Indians used. Climbing around is inconclusive as there are several possibilities. One cave has a table-like boulder in the middle that could have been used for meals, with an alcove behind it for sleeping. Looking up to see where these house-sized rocks broke off the valley wall, I don't spot any telltale dots of white granite, only the uniform gray of the slow-growing lichen that covers the wall and the rocks in this area. These boulders have been here for a long time, perhaps centuries. The retreating glaciers probably didn't drop them here because the edges of the boulders haven't been rounded by the tumbling and grinding of ice. Either water worked its way behind the rocks and a big freeze pried them loose from the side of the mountain, or perhaps water and a sizeable earthquake shook the valley because it looks like a great many rocks came down all at once.

In front of the caves is a large, flat slab of rock with several round mortar holes that were used by the Natives for grinding acorns. The inner surfaces of the hard granite are still smooth to the touch, the result of the preparation of food more than a century and a half ago.

Hikers have to share the trail from here to Mirror Lake with horses, but the recent rain has washed away many of the steaming piles of plop and the pungent pools of urine and has dispersed the smell and horseflies. Mirror Lake isn't much of a lake anymore. The Park Service used to dredge the lake for sand to spread on winter roads, but the dredging was halted when it was seen as interrupting the natural evolution of the lake. As a result, sedges and rushes began growing on the edges, then willows and grasses moved in as the soil of the lake bed dried out. Now bushes and young trees like aspen and cottonwood are settling down. Soon there will be ponderosa pines and finally a forest of red fir, with no evidence of Mirror Lake left behind. Sadly, it's the only lake in the valley.

By Curry Village, on the shady south side of the valley, I walk around the apple orchard and notice that every tree has a numbered metal tag on it. The orchard dates from the late 1800s, when J. C. Lamon, the first year-round settler, lived here. There's another orchard over by the schoolhouse. The tag numbers start with the trees by Curry and end with tree no. 126 in the far corner by Stoneman Meadow. I ask a ranger walking by about them. She says the numbers help them monitor the health of the trees and that some of the varieties only exist here. A crew of volunteers is coming this weekend to pick the apples so they don't attract more bears into the valley.

How does an apple taste? The question seems simple, but the answer is not. I've eaten a dozen varieties of apple, some that were tart, some sweet, but I haven't tasted the apple in front of me. What does a ponderosa tree feel like? Not any ponderosa, but this one, just beyond the orchard on the right side of the paved trail that goes to Happy Isles. I want to experience what is here now rather than say that because I've tasted an apple before there's no need to taste any others, because all apples are not alike. All ponderosa trees are not the same. Even I am not who I was yesterday. I've changed because of yesterday's experiences. My eating this apple today may be a transforming moment or it may simply be a pleasurable one. The apple may have a worm that will make me gag, but I won't know that unless I pick it and bite.

I stand motionless and try to breathe in autumn, breathe in everything that makes up this distinctive mountain air. The smells of brown leaves and dried cattails, the pungence of bay laurel and pine with a hint of oak and cherry, flow through the valley as the breeze brushes over the meadows. The air picks up aromas from the Merced River when it swings that way, and adds trail dust and warmth as the breeze flows over the canyon walls basking in sunlight. For much of the day I remain in this state of mindfulness . . . not that I'm fingering meditation beads or muttering prayers and causing people to scurry off the trails with trepidation as I approach. It's more that I feel open to everything and everyone. There are no plans that can't be changed. I head off without knowing where I'll end up or what will capture my attention. Sometimes there's a bird I don't recognize and I'll sit for many minutes watching it. Or a view up the valley will mesmerize me and I'll lie down on the riverbank and spend the entire afternoon drifting in and out of sleep as small, curious animals sneak up to investigate.

Beyond Curry Village, on the boardwalk that goes over the marsh-like fen, I listen for an hour to the water meandering and gurgling between bunches of horsetail, one of the ancient plants in the valley, like the ferns and lichen, that continues to exist much as it always has. The Ahwahnechees believed that the fairy-like creatures they called Nenakutu lived in the fen. Beyond this, the old cabin that was half-sunk in the marsh when I came through in February now floats in a sea of stone with its roof and walls intact, a sleight of hand trick pulled off by a massive rockslide that came down from Glacier Point.

Back at camp people have set up a three-foot-square chessboard on the ground with beer and wine bottles as the chess pieces. A half-gallon merlot jug is the king piece on one side, and a half-gallon California blush is the queen on the other. A variety of Rolling Rock, Anchor Steam, Henry Weinhard, and Sierra Nevada beer bottles make up the pawns, one Jack Daniels bottle stands in as a rook, and a Minute Maid orange juice bottle poses as a mystery piece. The thirty-four climbers gathered around the camp's twenty-foot-tall Columbia Boulder are trying to conquer its extremely difficult, overhanging Midnight Lighting route. No one is having any success today, even with cheers of encouragement from the crowd. After a dozen climbers fall off the rock like electrocuted squirrels, leaving white chalk handprints behind, I head for the camp bathroom. Ron Kauk—the climbing Adonis who moves over the rock like a dancer and one of the few people who can do that route—comes in and tinkles in the next stall. So he is human.

Quite a number of German and Japanese climbers are in camp, along with a few French and Spanish sprinkled in. Frank juggles lacrosse balls while riding his unicycle around camp. Three people play hacky-sack by the Search and Rescue tent. Others are doing laundry in plastic buckets, and two climbers take turns honing their balancing skills by walking a slack cord tied between two trees.

At twilight I celebrate with the Ahwahnechees in mind, who viewed the acorn harvest as the end of one year and the start of the next. It's also Rosh Hashanah, the Jewish festival of the New Year. Two ancient tribes who never knew of the other's existence celebrated the New Year together, separated by half the world but united by the agricultural cycle. This leads to a notion I hadn't considered: new life can start only after the death of the old. After harvest, the land and trees must lay fallow, let go of the bounty of summer, and endure an empty season as they prepare for new life. I, too, have to let go of my dead if I am to grow.

Around the evening campfire with Matt and Steve, the flickering light reveals frustration in their faces. They're back from attempting to climb Washington Column, having fallen several times with rope saves. We talk about what went wrong, where, and why. I feel drawn to share with them, so I talk about what I had seen today, but this seems so tame compared to the physical risks they took that I do not speak of the deeper discoveries going on, deciding to share more after I hike the impressive Pohono Trail in a day or so. Tomorrow they will try Washington again rather than attempt an easier climb. They don't know if they will make it or how they will get back down once they reach the top, but they figure they'll find out in due time and deal with it then. For them success is in the trying, not the standing on top.

The next afternoon I head for Happy Isles collecting acorns, dogwood leaves, and manzanita berries along the way, picking up pieces of the forest, river, and mountain. These knick-knacks and totems of power spur my memory of events here. I gather them together along with a feather for Ev. Remembering the mourning ceremony that the Ahwahnechees held every autumn, I climb onto a flat, thirty-foot wide rock that I call the altar stone and put the offerings on a boulder in the middle, then pour a measure of water to the four directions to celebrate this year's harvest, giving thanks for the goodness of the past and acknowledging its sorrows. I give thanks for the time I had with Evelyn, although it was not long enough; I'm grateful that I can carry her memory in the world. I give thanks for the gift of life and the simple joys of Yosemite's sunshine, air, and water. Closing my eyes, I let go of the past and listen to the wind on the mountains, smelling the rich earth beneath the trees and feeling the warmth of the sun on my skin. When time seems full I look up for my red-tailed hawk, then come down off the altar and wander along trails that hours later somehow lead me back to camp.

Around 10:00 p.m. Matt and Steve stagger in after their sixteen-hour successful climb up Washington Column. They fell again but nothing broke. And coming down the climbers' gully on the back side of North Dome, Matt says, "was hellish." I offer congratulations. They beam and head off for a hot shower and lots of something to eat before they collapse in exhaustion. I turn in, having waited for their return but knowing that there will be no more sharing tonight. From the warmth of my sleeping bag spread on the open ground I watch the stars journey across the frosty night, thankful for their company.

South Rim Hike—the Pohono Trail

Before first light in the morning I walk across the frozen, crunching meadow to the bottom of Sentinel Rock to begin the Pohono Trail hike. This will take me east up the Four Mile Trail to Glacier Point, west on the Pohono along the southern rim of the valley to Inspiration Point, down into the west end of the valley by Bridalveil Fall, and back to camp—twenty-five miles and ten hours. I've hiked parts of this trail before but never the whole thing. I don't even know if anyone ever attempts to do this. Most people get someone to drive them up to Glacier Point where they either hike down the Four Mile Trail to the valley floor or take the Panorama Trail to Nevada and Vernal Falls.

Overnight temperatures have dipped into the mid-thirties. Word around camp is that a winter storm is moving in, with heavy snow expected down to tent level. I'm layered in three sweaters and jackets and relish the crisp air and the bright stars, anticipating that the south side of the valley will remain in shade for most of the hike. This shade, combined with hiking four thousand feet higher in elevation, means that it will stay cold. I keep forgetting that temperatures in the mountains drop a few degrees every thousand feet higher in elevation, and then wonder why I still can't take my coat off. With luck it may reach the fifties by the time I come down into the valley at the other end.

Halfway up the valley wall the trail makes a big turn to face Sentinel Rock and the entire western end of the valley opens up. Sitting with my legs hanging over the edge, I savor the panoramic view of El Capitan, the Rockslides, and the narrow canyon leading out of Yosemite to El Portal. The upper half of Sentinel Rock is so close that a paper airplane could sail over to it, and I wonder if it's possible to hike over to the top of Sentinel from the back side. I'll take a look when I go by. At Union Point nearby an Irishman lived in a hut in the late 1800s and had this view every day. Some said he was crazy. Others thought he was building his own toll trail to the top, which is how most of the pioneer trails began. I think he found where his heart needed to be and stayed put. East of Union Point is Moran Point, with its own astonishing views, named for the painter, Thomas Moran, who came and made sketches of the valley on his travels through the west.

PEOPLE, BY DATE OF THEIR
FIRST VISIT TO YOSEMITE

1851   Lafayette Bunnell, arrived with the Mariposa Battalion, wrote the earliest descriptions of the place and its people

1855   Galen Clark, came to the mountains for his health, ran a way station on the Wawona Road, first Park Guardian

1863   Albert Bierstadt, early German Romantic painter of the valley

1868   John Muir, mountaineer, writer, mystic, speaker on the wonders of the valley, helped form the Sierra Club and gain federal protection for Yosemite

1895   Gabriel Sovulewski, most of the Yosemite trails in place by 1930 were built under his supervision

1916   Ansel Adams, master black-and-white photographer

1930   Carl Sharsmith, alpine botanist

My trail leaves the switchbacks and winds up a steep wooded ravine where 150-foot trees occasionally lose their footing on the sixty-degree slope and go crashing down the side of the mountain, taking other trees and parts of the trail with them. Like Basho on the pilgrim trails in southern Japan, I walk with only the goal of being present to nature, pausing now and then to listen to the quiet of the breeze swaying through the trees and the tiny streams trickling over the trail. The valley floor gets smaller and smaller as I climb thousands of feet higher, taking care not to slip off the foot-wide dirt path. I hike slowly up this canyon under the trees, delighting in this moment filled with sights, sounds, and scents.

Near the top I come upon the place where I turned back on my hike in February. The trail was there, as I thought, but instead of going straight ahead it hugged the contours of the cliff. I had been standing on a snow bridge when I decided to turn around, and only the cohesive power of the snow kept me from dropping into the valley. A cold shiver creeps up from my heels when I realize how quickly my life would have ended. I cross over and hurry on. Then I come back, curious to see what I would have landed on had the snow given way. A couple of hundred feet down there is a jagged outcrop that would have stopped my falling body and hidden it for a long time before anyone found me. I try to imagine the splayed position of my broken body and my frozen, surprised expression. Long drop, big plop. I laugh, and the gallows humor calms me. I want to confront my feelings of death and undo the fear so that the next time I hike through I will see only this view of the entire valley and the overhang near Glacier Point that people dance on and have their photograph taken. On the other side of the valley the rising sun has warmed the highlands and melted enough snow so that Yosemite Falls now has a thin liquid rainbow pouring down in front of its white-frosted wall.

The trail continues up through a dark pine glen with a thick carpet of aromatic needles, crosses over Glacier Point, and reaches the junction with the trail headed west toward Taft Point. By Sentinel Dome two white-tailed ptarmigans are feeding on the side path that goes to the top of the dome, Muir's second favorite viewing spot in the valley. Taking it as a sign, I detour and hike to the top of the dome, where a lone Jeffrey pine, twisted and gnarled by the strong wind and harsh weather in this exposed spot, once grew out of a crack in the rock. It managed to live a long life when other trees weren't able to even find a rooting. One year I took black and white photos of Evelyn standing by the Jeffrey's craggy, bare branches after it had died, using a red filter to create Ansel Adams'–type photographs that caught Ev's own strength of spirit.

Back on the rim trail I look for a non-life-threatening way to get over to Sentinel Rock, but don't see one. Because this trail is on the north side of the mountain crest, the sun still hasn't made it over the top to warm the land even though half the valley floor is now in sunlight. Frost adorns the bushes in the pocket meadows with sparkling crystals that collect and slowly melt on my hands as I walk through. When the trail swings back to the edge of Yosemite's cliffs I walk along with no fear of the trail crumbling, figuring that the trail makers knew what they were doing one hundred years ago. Of course, the weathering of the seasons since then could make this an iffy conclusion. Even with a vertical drop of four thousand feet just a foot away, I give little thought that the cliff will suddenly give way and I'll go falling to my death. Walking along with nothing visually to one side except a mile of empty air, I feel light and suspended between earth and heaven. As I approach Taft Point, surprised at how far it protrudes over the valley like the prow of a ship, I fail to notice a turn in the trail and step into open space. With a lurch I twist around and catch enough scrub manzanita to pull myself back onto the trail.

As I near Taft Point at 10:30 a.m., four black triangles shoot into the air through fissures in the ground, circle around, and shoot up again. The disks turn out to be ravens that are having a great time riding the wind as it pushes across the valley, hits the wall, and blasts up through the crevices like a roller coaster ride. Other than sightings of single ravens around the valley, I've also watched them work as a pair when gathering food from a road one day by the Housekeeping Camp. One acted as a sentinel and warned of oncoming cars while the other one picked apart whatever dead creature was in the road. I've also heard that they like to collect shiny objects and show off their collections to each other. Steering clear of the catapulting birds and the gaping fissures in the ground, some that drop for hundreds of feet, I reach the crest of Taft Point and lean on the railing, seeing the valley from a new perspective and amazed again at the sight before me. Hearing voices, I peer over the railing at two climbers, who are teaching their dates how to climb. Today's lesson seems to involve hanging eighty feet over the edge of Taft in a sling and swinging back and forth in order to show them it's safe. Their dates do not look convinced, as they hold on tight.

After Taft the trail descends into Bridalveil Canyon, down to the creek at the bottom that flows over Bridalveil Fall. A musky scent lets me know that some large animal is around. A couple of minutes later a deer bounds across the trail as if fleeing something, but the scent wasn't from a deer. I've learned at least that much in my time here. Something else is in the woods nearby. I listen closely, hear nothing alarming, only birds, wind, squirrels chattering to each other, and the occasional caw of a raven.

At the bottom of the canyon, eighteen-foot-wide Bridalveil Creek rushes down from left to right in the steep and slick water-polished channel. Its bridge is still gone from the spring flood, which presents a problem. Should I turn around and go back? I do what I always do now: I take the risk with the chance that I will tumble into the river, slide down toward Bridalveil Fall, and be dead like that fabled Indian maiden. I no longer believe in my invincibility because of Evelyn's unexpected death, but part of me also no longer cares what happens. I also know that I need to take risks if I'm going to stay alive.

Fashioning a staff out of a fallen branch, I hop on boulders to get across the creek and use the stick to keep my balance on the polished rocks. Partway over my stick breaks, but momentum throws me forward. I leap from boulder to boulder to keep from falling into the water until I reach the far bank. Turning around, I notice with annoyance and surprise the bottom half of my staff sticking up in the middle of the stream.

The electricity of the impromptu creek hopping continues to zing through my body during the half hour hike up the steep incline of the canyon to Dewey Point. Today is the feast day of Francis of Assisi, who valued simplicity of living, love of nature, and love for all living things as creatures of God. His preaching to the birds is something I understand outdoors, although here Steller's jays would insist on doing the talking. Rounding a bend and thinking of his Canticle of Creation, with its moving ode to Brother Sun and Sister Moon, I meet a massive black dog. Its owners are nearby, which calms my sudden panic, and I let him slobber my hands for Francis's sake, although as a former paperboy I'm not fond of big dogs. Then sensing either my growing fear or my disgust over his stringy slobber on my hands, he begins to growl. His owners catch up, collect him, and apologetically hurry on.

I reach Dewey Point at 12:30, eat lunch, and stare at Clouds Rest at the east end of the valley, marveling that I survived a hike to its top. On the north side of the valley the ancient ridges, where the mountains folded when they were still molten and pliable to geologic forces, are visible. The covering of bushes and grass looks soft to the touch, although it'd probably feel bristly if my hands were large enough to brush over them. North Dome looks like a bump below the huge mound of Indian Ridge, but El Capitan is still impressive and I always look for it to get my bearings. One legend says that the Native Americans called El Cap "Crane Mountain" because cranes flying by would use it to check their direction. Some say the truth goes deeper, that the spirituality of the land is written large and the Sierra Nevada is part of a long spiritual highway that connects the length of the Americas, with El Cap as one of its beacons of energy.

There are additional stops at Crocker and Stanford Points to check their views. Finally at Stanford, the white plume of Bridalveil Fall is visible. Who was Crocker, what was Stanford's connection with the valley, and which Dewey was the point named after? I have my hunches, but as much as I'd like to know this history I don't think it matters. I wish more for a trail guide of Native American history around the valley. They lived here for thousands of years and must have countless stories to tell. Yet even wanting this, I appreciate the small number of historical signs. Yosemite is not a museum of the past but a living place where I can encounter nature directly.

I cross Meadow Brook, which flows over Silver Strand Falls somewhere in the bushes above me and continues downhill over Washburn Slide somewhere below, to Artist Creek with clumps of Indian Paintbrush hanging on. Even though it's still cold and I'm bundled in layers of jackets, I'm thoroughly enjoying this jaunt, feeling connected to the contours of the mountain, the trees, and the creeks; I'm flowing with the natural sounds of the day.

A patch of blue appears on the trail ahead. I investigate. It's a pile of blue feathers, so it's the remains of a bird. My guess is that a hawk was involved, although it could have been an owl because they do eat small birds, plucking them and swallowing them whole. The indigestible material is coughed up later as brown pellets of skin and bone. It could even have been a Pygmy owl. Although they weigh only two ounces, the size of a small bird, they are known to eat such things. My bet is that a hawk swooped out of the sky, surprised a Steller's jay on the ground, and took the carcass to its nest.

A haunting shriek rips through the air. What was that! Perhaps the hawk shouting its victory through a bloody beak. I become aware that I wasn't as aware of my surroundings as I had thought, having succumbed to the pleasantness of hiking through these bucolic woods. What I thought was mindfulness was also partially mindless, and the illusion of my closeness to the mountain drops away. Yet this failure doesn't feel like I have to go back to the start and begin again. It's more like a moment of clarity, like windshield wipers on a misty day or a Zen monk whacking my shoulders with a bamboo stick. The mystery here is that the mountain is a whole but it is also many parts. With the cry I realize there is more to this mountain than what I perceive.

A few minutes of hiking later, the Old Wawona Stagecoach Road pooches in with its history. The road was built over the old Native American trail that the Mariposa Battalion followed in on horses, which is what brought Lafayette Bunnell to this spot on the valley wall 160 years ago. He was overcome with awe at his first view of the valley and his enthusiastic reactions were set against the indifference of his military companions, who were tired from the trip and wary of being ambushed by the Native Americans they had come to take away from their homes. They likely just wanted to get down to the valley floor, set up camp in the snow, and sleep. Unfortunately, the view from Old Inspiration Point is now blocked by mature trees. I follow the remains of the stagecoach trail down to the base of Bridalveil Fall, pausing only at Artist Point to imagine Thomas Hill standing here painting his famous view. I'm tired and it's still four miles back to camp, but thankfully all on flat valley floor.

Back at camp, Matt and Steve are gone. They weren't sure if they were going to try another climb or head home because of the approaching winter storm. Their missing tent leaves a place of emptiness behind. I didn't get a chance to say good-bye to them; I liked their presence. Their departure reminds me of the transitory quality of life, especially in the mountains. The beauty of the day can shift from warm sun to freezing rain in less than an hour. A massive earthquake can wipe out the trails, making it impossible to hike from the valley into the highlands. A flash flood can roar through and sweep away all the buildings, campsites, and supporting infrastructure, making the valley uninhabitable for years.

I also realize something else. The wonderful feelings I experienced today cannot be preserved because they are living moments. Once I leave the valley these moments of great importance will fade like picked flowers. They will cease to breathe and turn into memory, as all experiences stiffen after their moment and can only be remembered fondly as something that once happened. Even though I am here, no, *because* I am here every moment is special because it does not last more than a few hours. The red and orange autumn leaves in front of the blue Royal Arches that I marveled at yesterday morning might never glow like that again, so I should not hurry past on my way to see something else. I may never hike the Pohono Trail again in such nice weather.

Matt and Steve are gone and I will probably never see them again. Two nights ago I had the chance to speak more about my journey and I did not, thinking I would have time later. But in the sharing I did with them I realized how much I miss sharing in relationships.

The solitude and presence of today's hike has so permeated me that when Anika and Georg show up in camp, putting their tent where Matt and Steve's had been, I stumble over my words trying to introduce myself. From Austria, they have just finished six weeks of hiking the length of the John Muir Trail, starting in Southern California. They should be interesting to talk to, and probably have great stories to tell from their time on a trail I'd like to explore. He has blond dreadlocks and tattoos. She has cute eyes and a lip ring. I think she's flirting with me, wanting someone other than Georg to talk to. Suddenly I want to flirt as well, and the feeling catches me off guard. But I still have trouble forming complete sentences so I nod good-night and turn in. I fall asleep remembering the encounters of this day.

Embracing the Stone Season

How fiercely, devoutly wild is Nature in the midst of her
beauty-loving tenderness.

—John Muir, *My First Summer in the Sierra*

Winter settles into the Sierra Nevada and the trails in Yosemite's
backcountry harden with ice. The golden hues of autumn that
have hung on finally let go and turn gray. All the trees that are
going to lose their leaves have done so, making El Capitan seem
even taller and more honorable. The powdering of snow over the
valley's walls accents the landscape's features hidden the rest of
the year, and the season of stone begins.

The valley's new openness to the sky conveys a sense of 150
years ago, when the settlers first wandered around in awe through
largely treeless meadows. There's a feeling of the sky reaching down
and embracing the land, of heaven and earth meeting in a trinity
of granite, water, and air, of the forces of life and death comming-
ling. As soon as I enter the valley I find what is missing in my life.
Every time I return I realize how much of its stunning scenery I've
forgotten. Every time I return I hike further down the unmapped
trails, beyond my need to understand to where I simply accept.

The sun peeks above Half Dome to the east, sending rays of light across the tops of trees to the west. A broad band of yellow slowly descends through branches to touch the darkness at their feet. This line of dawn advances eastward across the grass of Cook's Meadow toward where I sit in the shadows, lighting up the meadow's sheet of white frost and melting it into glistening dew. Hollow milkweed pods, standing dry on their stiff brown stalks, catch the flame of the yellow sun and glow like tiny paper lanterns hanging on poles. When the edge of dawn reaches the tips of my shoes, I walk back into the cold shade of night to get hot coffee at Degnan's store.

Sitting on the outdoor patio, I savor the warmth of the cup in my hands, trying to be present to everything that is happening in this moment, listening to Steller's jays squawking in the trees, staking out their territory or just being ornery. Brewer's blackbirds chirr and hop around the table, hoping for handouts, but they don't seem awake enough to be serious about it. Squirrels chirp to their friends to come out and play, then chase each other up the trees and over Degnan's roof. Deer nuzzle leaves on the ground to the side, looking for acorns they missed on previous days.

Through the dark woods the glow of dawn approaches a second time. The cold brushes past as the warmth of the present approaches. When sunlight reaches the bare branches above me I again head east, into the darkness that still embraces Ahwahnee Meadow. There I sit and wait as my third dawn of the day approaches, the light moving faster now and pushing the last of night's shadows up the blue stone of the Royal Arches and into the sky.

Heading west in this early light I think of the past and the people whose lives and writings have awakened me to the frailty and transcendent beauty of the environment: Chief Teneiya,

Lafayette Bunnell, and John Muir, of course, but also David Brower, Wendell Berry, Rachel Carson, Sigurd Olson, and Gary Snyder. I hike up to El Capitan's nose and touch this rock of witness, offering thanks for its inspiration. Climbing the talus slope on the left side for half an hour to explore what's there, I notice a narrow ledge that goes out onto El Cap's face. Hugging the wall with my chest and reaching for any cracks I can grasp with my fingertips, I slide out as far as possible until the inside edges of my shoes barely hold the tapering ledge. Looking down, I'm five hundred feet above the valley floor. Giddy over finally feeling like a climber and seeing the sharp drop that climbers see, I crane my neck back carefully, look up the wall, and spot two climbers a thousand feet overhead, setting their gear as they prepare to move higher.

After a few minutes in my tenuous position, a falling rock thwacks nearby and I decide my time here is done. Sliding off El Cap and back to solid ground, I retreat to the bridge by the meadow where I see a perfect reflection of El Capitan on the river's water. "How beautiful," I think, then realize that El Cap is backward, and an inner stillness flows over me. In this instant I realize there is a flip side to all my thoughts; not negative, but reversed. There will always be more than what I see, always more than what I understand, always something wild and unpredictable that will show up to unsettle my firm conclusions and push me to look further. I feel like the scientists who have been able to locate only 4 percent of the matter in the universe, leaving them to speculate about the other 96. I thought my journey into nature's wildness would help me explore the workings of the wilderness within me, and it has. But my journey inward has also helped me understand nature's reality. The two journeys have been linked.

In the meadows at dusk, El Capitan, Cathedral Rocks, and Half Dome glow with the rich orange, red, and purple of the sunset. The visual feast of warmth offsets the damp coldness that has been edging the signs of joy returning to my life with a sense of vulnerability.

Back at camp I meet Bob and Jason. They're from the Sawtooth Mountains of Idaho, and Bob, now in his forties, began climbing in Yosemite twenty years ago but hasn't been back for awhile, having spent years working on fishing boats off Alaska, getting married, and having kids. Both worked on Friday then drove all night, arrived at 3:00 a.m., slept in their car, then got into line to secure a place in camp. After the ranger station opened at 8:30, they set up their tent and headed to El Cap. The plan was to haul their gear up five pitches on fixed ropes, then climb to that point and stay the night. But they were tired from not having slept the night before and feeling sick from colds they had caught from their kids, and they could only move their two hundred pounds of gear up 150 feet. Then it was dark and they stumbled back to camp to sleep. But all their gear was hanging on El Cap, so they had an empty tent, one poncho, and an old, flat climbing mat they rescued out of the trash. They still didn't get any sleep as temperatures went down into the low forties.

Sunday morning they got up, went back to El Cap, struggled to get the gear one pitch higher, called it quits at midday, and came back to camp to sleep. Jason mumbled, "It was like we got here and said, 'Big Wall. Must climb!'" Bob added, "It was like Dumb and Dumber Go Climbing." Yet happy to be in the valley, Jason brings out Bodinger beer and Bob passes around his whiskey. We get warm and toasty and talk into the night until we lose our grasp of consonants. Tomorrow, after a decent night's sleep, they will try a shorter route.

Ostrander Lake Hike

At dawn, a dark brown ten-point buck stands vigilant in the shadows under the oak trees by the Native grinding rock west of camp. One warm autumn day Evelyn and I helped our friends Molly and Francesco renew their vows by this rock. Molly had been struggling with a brain tumor for a number of years and they wanted to reaffirm their commitment to each other no matter what the future would bring. Evelyn sang a beautiful song that day. Six months later Ev was dead.

On the left side of Cook's Meadow, again white with heavy frost, four coyotes are playing tag, chasing each other around at full speed, nipping at heels, and doubling back to send their bodies tumbling over each other. In the far right corner a number of deer are eating peacefully. By me on this edge of the meadow half a dozen photographers are bent over their cameras and tripods taking close-up pictures of elegantly crystallized dew on the leaves of plants, oblivious to everything going on around them. At some signal the coyotes quiet down and trot single file through a low depression in the meadow toward the deer, hidden from everyone's view. When they emerge on the other side they break into a sprint and the deer race for the river. The old and young begin to lag behind as the coyotes get closer. The chase enters the trees and one buck comes back to battle the coyotes but the encounter moves out of view. Leaving the photographers behind, I run that way and hear crashing in the brush and the river, but by the time I arrive the battle has moved elsewhere.

My adventure today is to hike to the Ostrander Ski Hut in the backcountry, starting along the road that goes to Glacier Point. Ever since reading Howard Weamer's article on the place I've wanted to take this trip. He wrote about the solitude he discovered when riding out snowstorms alone in the hut, as well as skiing across the pristine backcountry by himself. He also wrote about the wide-ranging discussions on science, philosophy, art, and religion he'd have in the evenings with ski campers from all walks of life.

The hike is not long, only twelve miles round trip, and the day is warming nicely to the upper forties in the bright sun. The first third of the hike is relatively flat and Lost Bear Meadow shows up on the left. The story behind the name is that a pioneer girl got lost there one day and was eventually found, but she claimed that a bear she had seen was still lost. The rest of the hike to the hut is gradually uphill, gaining fifteen hundred feet in elevation, with the usual gathering of purple finches and white-breasted nuthatches chirping away. The sound of acorn woodpeckers knocking on dead trees echoes through the woods, while golden-mantled ground squirrels search the forest floor, looking for things to eat.

Purple lupine is still blooming, which is surprising because it's so late in the year and most other flowers have long turned to seed but it's only three inches high and probably one of the shorter species in Yosemite. Coming over a rise I walk into a graveyard of white skeletons fifty feet tall. An entire grove of dead, barkless trees has faded to chalk-white like dinosaur bones in the sun. Did fire, disease, or something else cause this? I explore the grove, looking for clues. A few of the trees on the edge still have their bark without any sign of flames, so it may not have been a fire. Forest fires did hit two areas along the trail, but those groves have burn marks and are in various stages of recovery. The newest grove, from a fire six years ago, has three-foot pines growing in the burned-out area along with a variety of low-lying ground cover that has fought its way back. The older burn from a decade ago has new pines that are twelve feet high.

An hour into my hike I spot a small pile of orange and purple something and think of the blue pile of feathers from a Steller's jay that I found in October. But what bird or animal is purple and orange? With a stick I gingerly poke at the remains, expecting to disturb something gooey and disgusting like an animal's intestines, but it's the viscera of a sugar pine cone that has been completely picked apart by a squirrel. The orange of each prong is accenting the purple wing that had been attached to a seed. As the trail moves back under the trees, odd noises, from either an exotic bird or some animal in pain, begin coming from the woods ahead. Around the bend two people are hooting loudly at a large bird that I only glimpse in the trees. They see me and stop, looking embarrassed. We exchange pleasantries and I continue on but without hearing any more hooting from John and Cheryl.

More than two hours after starting out I reach the Ostrander Hut and the nearby lake. The cabin, constructed of broad wooden beams and stone boulders reminiscent of the LeConte Memorial on the valley floor, sits on a glacial moraine, which is what holds the lake together. The hut, with its bunks and wooden table in the middle, is closed now, being a snow place, and it looks comfy through the windows. The lake is not large but it is striking, bordered by the granite of Horse Ridge on one side and the granite of Horizon Ridge on another. In the 1930s Chiura Obata, a professor at UC-Berkeley, painted a watercolor that captures the spare beauty of this scene.

The lake is also the headwater for Bridalveil Creek, although it's not providing much water now. Playing Colossus for a moment, I straddle the three-foot-wide stream, put hands on hips, and give a hearty laugh, knowing that what's flowing underneath will soon become Bridalveil Fall and that I'm in complete control of everything. "Ha, HAH!" Okay, moment over, because John and Cheryl are arriving, finally making it up the trail with their heavier gear. We have a better conversation this time, discuss camping areas, how one might hike cross-country over the ridge and hook up with the trail from Glacier Point, and the pros and cons of jumping into the lake with its snowmelt water. I elect not to, but Cheryl thinks she might later on during the warmest part of the day. She's either nuts or Finnish, like my friend Bernie.

Heading back down, I take a side trip to the top of Horizon Ridge and look over the area behind Half Dome, where water gathers for Illilouette, Nevada, and Vernal Falls. The main attractions are Red Peak, Mount Clark, and Mount Starr King, named for the Unitarian pastor who extolled Yosemite's beauty to his national audience in the late 1800s. It's a stark, exposed landscape of light gray granite and small blue lakes where life is tenuous. Trees are able to grow only in scattered pockets on the stone slopes. I'm at the elevation of the mountain peaks that stretch to the horizon and the sound flowing over the stone landscape is profound and still. I don't know how else to describe it. Without trees and plants and animals moving about, the air seems empty of sounds. It feels light, as if the weight of gravity has been cut in half. And it's filled with presence that draws me to walk into it with reverence and listen to the rock, the sky, and the water.

Turning around, I look over the basin for Bridalveil Creek. On this side of the divide, broad green forests and fertile meadows cover the contours of the land all the way over to the Mariposa Grove of giant sequoias. My life feels like this: walking the ridge between grief and life, unsure where I belong.

Back on the trail I find tracks that weren't here two hours ago. If a bear made them, then that bear only has front paws. It was probably a mountain lion, which sets its back feet where its front feet have been. I get excited, knowing that she is probably watching me, and will continue to watch as I hike back down. Perhaps I can catch a glimpse of her tan fur or the flow of her powerful muscles in a spot of sunlight as she glides through the shadows under the line of trees.

Back in the valley, I stop at the photo studio to look at Ansel Adams's black-and-white photos of the area I just traversed, trying to figure out how he created them—where he stood, what camera settings he used, the time of day and season, so that I can duplicate his results. And I see Dana. I noticed her in September when she answered a difficult question kindly during an evening presentation she gave on photography. She's my height, with dark hair and brown eyes, a delicious lower lip, gazelle-like legs, and the sinuous look of an outdoorswoman. I debated going up and asking her out for coffee but was afraid that I'd end up babbling about grief and that wouldn't have been fair to her. I still don't feel ready, and instead go back outside.

Relishing the warmth of the sun in the cool air, I head to Tenaya Canyon to sit in Fern Grotto for an hour, remembering Ev and the friends who have died over the years, wondering why they had to die so young. There may never be an acceptable answer for this. I watch birds soar over the canyon and listen to the quiet of the mountains and the sounds of the trees swaying in the breeze, trying to believe that everything happens for a reason.

I climb up through one of the thirty-foot waterfalls to the top, then walk on a narrow trail that heads toward Half Dome, wondering where I'm going to end up because this trail isn't on my map. Coming out of the bushes ahead is a large bearded man in a flannel shirt and broad-rimmed hat carrying a big wooden staff. He looks like he's been living in the mountains for a couple of years, yet seems friendly enough by the way he's moving toward me. There's no place to hide, anyway, so when we get close I ask about the path. "Deer trail," he says, a few teeth missing. "Goes over to the face of Half Dome." Out of words, he moves on. I glance back once to see him heading up the canyon on the Native path toward Tenaya Lake, a route that has frequent rockslides. When my path disappears under manzanita bushes I scramble down a ravine to a regular trail.

On the way back to the main valley two bears are on the wooded slope below North Dome. This is where I would have landed had I slipped off the dome in May. The younger bear is digging around in the bushes, scratching itself, and finding a lot of objects to play with. The older, heavier one, probably the mother, sits and watches. I figure any creature that plays has some level of consciousness going on, and possibly a soul as well, although as a child I was taught that only people have souls. Yet animals have exhibited concern for others, even sacrificing themselves for members of different species. To me this is the mark of a soul, even though admittedly there are some humans who wouldn't do this to help their own.

Native Americans were content to sketch their theology in broad strokes, focusing on the essential points without getting into too many details, believing that everything has its own spirit and that each individual is part of the larger spirituality of the world. They saw all of creation as being interdependent and tried to live their lives in union with nature. Worship was ongoing and the Great Spirit lived with them, interacting with what they were doing. Chief Seattle of the Suquamish tribe in Washington spoke of the rivers as being our brothers and regarded the peaks of the mountains, the juices of the meadows, the body heat of horses, and human beings as belonging to the same family.

In Spain, John of the Cross wrote of his connection to nature this way: "My Beloved is the mountains and lonely wooded valleys, strange islands, and resounding rivers, the whistling of love-stirring breezes, the tranquil night at the time of the rising dawn." Japanese Buddhists and Celtic Christians share a similar reverence for all life. They feel that God is present in everything created. The Sufis, believers in the mystical branch of Islam, regard the physical world as God's greatest creation. So my challenge is simple (paraphrasing William Blake): "To see the world in a grain of sand, and eternity in an hour." Each of these traditions assures me that life does not end in death.

It was once thought that with the right instruments scientists would be able to see the smallest particles that existed in nature and then build up from there our complete understanding of how the world works, putting the missing pieces into all the puzzles that have befuddled humanity since the dawn of human consciousness. Yet even with electron microscopes and particle accelerators twenty miles long scientists still can't see enough. It's as if they have walked to the edge of a great valley and looked down, expecting to see the answers to their long search but instead seeing nothing at the bottom—no trees, no rivers, no grand meadows. They were as likely to see the hot magma that formed these mountains sixty million years ago or the stars of the Milky Way in the place where the meadows should be. The answers they sought are not to be found in something specific, in one point of pure knowledge, but in the awareness of a cosmic mind behind all the facts, the designer of the mysteries, the Thought before thought, the Word in the beginning before words were spoken, the Great Spirit of the Ahwahnechees, the Heart that beats like a drum within the earth and sends the rain to nourish the land and all its creatures.

Blake challenges me to pay attention to nature's details when I'm outdoors. I've felt the truth of his insight at times: if I truly experience reality then the essence of the entire world can be perceived in even its smallest part, as in a grain of sand. In Yosemite I'm continually inspired. How this happens I can't say, and I don't ever want to get so exact that I can't see the beauty of nature anymore. Mark Twain always regretted knowing what lay beneath the swells in the water as he learned to guide riverboats down the Mississippi River because he no longer saw its beauty, only danger. Being able to see mystery and wonder around me is enough. I don't want to mess this up by thinking too much.

Part of me no longer cares why natural places affect me so deeply, and I'm not really concerned about what does or doesn't have a soul. If I say that every part of creation reveals something about nature's reality then I'm challenged to look at everything with respect and find insights. In the coyote there is cunning, wisdom, and playfulness. In the ouzel (the American dipper), a bird that swims under water, there is the celebration of the moment. Standing on top of Half Dome I feel its strength and endurance through the ages. The wild outdoors simply inspire me. But I do want to simplify my life so that I'm not worn out and frustrated at the end of every workday. I want to move at a pace that helps me notice what is around me and gives me the chance to interact with it. I want to live so that whenever I come back to the wilderness for a week, I don't have to sleep the first couple of days. This would make John Muir happy.

At dinner, Bob and Jason talk about the day's adventures. Enjoying their company, I forego my evening hike and listen to them. They climbed Serenity Crack behind the Ahwahnee Hotel and it was a joy, a long pure line with pitch after pitch of crack climbing that still has Jason buzzing with excitement. Crack climbing, they tell me, emphasizes using hands rather than mechanical gear. You insert your fingers into a crack and crimp them inside in order to get a hold and pull yourself up. You also stick the toes of your shoes into openings to help you move upward. If the crack is wide enough you can also insert your flat hand and expand it into a fist.

They pull out a dog-eared book and show me the route, how they climbed straight up to here, went around this bush, and then headed straight for the top. To keep his body supple and in shape Bob does Tai Chi, and when he climbs he puts a strip of athletic tape around each knuckle in a practiced fashion to protect it from the granite's sharp edges. I mention seeing a pair of sixty-year-olds with gray hair walking into camp today, replete with coils of climbing ropes hanging over their bronzed, muscled torsos as well as others in camp that are going bald. The thought that he could climb for a long time makes Bob smile. What impresses me is that he hasn't boasted of any of the grand climbs he's done, only made passing references. He does talk about the philosophy of Krishnamurti, though.

Jason, in his thirties, also climbs ice, which fascinates both of us. Ice climbers, he says, go up the streams of water that flow over cliffs and freeze. Part of the skill is knowing which ice is safe to climb. It used to be that one had to cut steps into the ice in order to get anywhere, but refinements in tools have created the crampons for walking up ice and axes for controlling one's balance. The crampon on each foot, he explains, can have as many as twenty-four spikes, ideal for gripping the ice and everything else in its way. The challenge is to endure freezing temperatures, falling ice, and changing weather conditions. Jason particularly likes the mixed-media routes that have a combination of rock and ice surfaces. One time the ice sheet he was climbing cracked off and he fell fifteen feet, with the heavy sheet of ice landing on top of him. He survived the fall and the impact of the ice, but one of his needle-sharp crampons gashed his leg and left a five-inch scar that he happily shows us. It looks gnarly, like he sewed it up with needle and thread from an old canvas tent repair kit.

I head out for the sunset. Approaching the river, I feel drawn to go beyond where I usually sit, to the bend that faces south instead of west, which will make it difficult to see the sunset's colors or to watch for my ouzel, who was absent last night at our usual meeting spot further down the river. I continue on, having learned to trust this inner voice. This is how I found the climbers' path going up to El Cap, the waterfalls in Fern Grotto, the family of deer sleeping in a pocket meadow by Eagle Peak, the remains of an early settlement by Black Spring in the west end, and Lost Lake, with its snakes on the backside of Half Dome. I leave the path for the river, where there are small rapids, consoling myself that at least I can listen to its sounds. I sit on the gravel beach between two-foot-tall bunches of sedge grass and there in the river is my ouzel, dancing in the water as ouzels do—hop hop dip, hop hop dip. Swim. Shake. Hop hop dip. The good smell of the river, filled with the scents of earth and granite, comes down on the breeze. My ouzel takes a bath and sings an enchanting tune.

When it flies off home I go down to the river's edge. Touching the water, I feel the coldness of its current run through my fingers. Winter is coming down from the highlands into the valley. Lifting my hand, the drops of water fall back to their earth in the Merced River as darkness settles around me. I think with sadness of the turning of the seasons and the death of the valley's plants and insects. I think of spring that will warm the land and usher in a new cycle of life. I think of Evelyn and how I struggled to find the desire to live without her, feeling that everything I loved was gone. I think of my own death and how fleeting my life would seem, no matter what I may do of note, in comparison to the epic struggles that have gone on in this valley for millennia. Instead of returning directly to camp I take the long way around, letting the water dry slowly on my hand, allowing my thoughts to settle to earth, feeling close to the valley and not wanting to lose touch with this.

Returning Home

The moon is looking down into the cañon, and how mar-
velously the great rocks kindle to her light! Every dome,
and brow, and swelling, . . . glows as if lighted with snow.

—John Muir, *Steep Trails*

Driving cautiously over the icy road, I keep climbing in elevation.
The road clings precariously to the side of the mountain, lining
my nervousness with an edge of fear. Going down a steep descent
I sense that I am getting close to my destination and look up to
see the winter beauty of Yosemite Valley spread out before me:
El Capitan, Half Dome, and Bridalveil Fall all clothed in their
winter finery. Distracted by the vista, I speed too fast around a
bend and find myself heading for a two-thousand-foot drop. I
regain control and pull over to the side of the road, shaking from
what had almost happened.

After staring at the wonder ahead for five minutes, I drive slowly
the rest of the way down. On the valley floor, no matter where I
look I see stunning images of beauty: snow-covered meadows,
green pine trees, mile-high granite cliffs, and icy blue rivers.

Muir used to complain about people taking the train to Yosemite because he felt that nothing could be experienced at forty miles per hour. He wished that people would ride horses for three days to reach the valley, or take several weeks and walk in. The same problem exists today because people who arrive by car still need a few days to slow down from the pace of modern life. Yet, no matter how we reach the valley, I think Muir would be pleased that we have come so that nature could work its magic on us.

The cycle of life has turned once: from seed rising out of frozen earth to budding plant and glorious flower to a return to brown stalk and seed waiting again in the frozen meadows for the melting of spring. Newborn fawns and baby wrens grew into the gangly adolescents of summer. Rivers swelled with spring's runoff and slowed again into the trickling, meandering creeks of autumn. Each month, Yosemite has been a different place. As the seasons progressed the light shifted and highlighted different granite monuments in the valley. Scents have changed and the valley has become a new creation. On occasion the mountains glowed with an ethereal light and vibrated with a resonance as clear as a glass bell. At other times the stone mountains have been as hard as iron, indifferent to the needs of any individual. Even though there doesn't seem to be much going on in December, the beautiful meadows are still here with coyotes, ravens, and deer. The rivers and waterfalls still talk, but now with their quieter winter voices. Dawns and sunsets continue to be full of colors, but muted ones. Black oak trees and sequoias endure the transition to harsh weather with nobility.

Overnight it snows, and in the morning the land is unified in a blanket of white so that it matches the color of the clouds and unhooks the valley from its moorings to earth, making it seem like it's floating in the sky. Dawn tries to break through the clouds but can't quite make it. Yet the filtered sun lights the sky and the snow-clad meadows with a luminous yellow glow that gives the cold air palpable warmth and inspires the hermit thrushes to sing. I brush off a log in Leidig Meadow and sit, looking west toward the single ponderosa pine I've become attached to. I still carry the burden of thinking that I always need to be doing something useful. This has been a hard habit to break. The morning sun warms the trees and I realize how fragrant these unproductive pine needles smell in the clean air, and how the valley resounds with the talk of waterfalls and creeks flowing through the valley. The banter of all the creatures of the valley is completely useless, and so is my delight in them. Yosemite's winter beauty changes every hour as the sun moves across the sky, inspiring me even when I thought I'd seen it all. Lights and shadows intermingle. Sounds change, too, as the breeze gathers strength, shifts direction, and releases. In the side chapels of the valley, where creeks trickle down, quiet etudes play to small audiences of squirrels, chickadees, and deer.

By early afternoon the clouds have thickened as a new storm heads toward the valley. The brighter colors of morning deepen into blues, purples, and grays, which lend heaviness to the meadows. I sit by the river and wait to be covered by falling snow. A white egret meditates a hundred yards downstream, a fluff of white suspended over the dark water, dividing the river's flow with one leg. By midafternoon snow begins coming down. Staying perfectly still, I let an inch accumulate on my shoulders, legs, and stocking cap. A bird mistakes me for a rock and lands on my head before realizing its mistake and flies off. The sun penetrates through the clouds enough to light the upper atmosphere in yellow. Below, in the meadow, the partially frozen river is still colored in shades of purple and gray, but now in between earth and sky the opaque sun paints the falling flakes in sparkling pastel dots of pink, orange, and blue.

Johannes Kepler used to sit outside and meditate on snow-flakes. He considered a wide number of causes for their design and concluded that their hexagonal shape was the natural form that soft objects take in nature when under pressure. He pointed to the hexagon that bees use to store food in their hives as supporting evidence. The Devil's Postpile, a few miles from Yosemite, is probably another example. Yet, although Kepler says form and function have dictated the six-sidedness of snowflakes, he couldn't help wondering if nature's playfulness wasn't also involved.

Tonight is the Winter Solstice. I stay up late to see if I can notice when the stars shift in the sky as the Northern Hemisphere turns back toward the sun but am unable to pick up the subtle movement or hear the sound of celestial gears shifting.

Upper Yosemite Falls Hike

In the morning I wake up shivering. I've finally reached the lower limit of my sleeping bag's ability to keep me warm. During the night the sky has cleared of clouds, and with that single change the temperature has dropped to twelve degrees. As temperatures slid, I pulled the drawstring tight on my bag so that only my nose was exposed, like a snorkel. When my head emerges outside the bag, the skin on my face instantly stiffens. I exhale and a three-foot plume of fog moves across the tent.

As I eat breakfast some deer nearby nibble at the hard ground. There aren't many of them around. There also aren't many tents in Camp 4. Only nude buckwheat holds on in the meadows, where moist air from the river keeps a layer of biting cold that penetrates my clothing. I keep moving to stay warm.

As the sun rises behind Glacier Point—gleaming yellow on the bare granite of North Dome—it illuminates the meadows with warm light. Over in Cook's Meadow, acorn woodpeckers hop up on the trunks of dead trees to pick out acorns they had stored there in the fall. Three young bucks hang out by Sentinel Bridge, looking for trouble, their breaths coming out in small puffs. The crow in a nearby tree repeatedly makes a gurgle noise. It's a funny sound, and each time the crow caws its tail goes down. By Swinging Bridge a squarish six-inch chunk of light gray granite that was washed downstream by the powerful rush of the spring flood sits on the edge of a reflecting pool of emerald green. Icy white lace edges the banks of the calm Merced River, and its tranquil water reflects the blue sky.

I start up the Yosemite Falls Trail. Today's high is expected to be in the twenties, with a chance for snow. The snow level is down to six thousand feet, which is about halfway up the trail. Clouds are already moving in. My plan is to see if a trail is open at the top and hike either to El Capitan or North Dome. On a break at the Columbia Rock viewing point I look over the snow-covered meadows. The black water of the rivers and creeks curves across the white landscape like Japanese brush strokes on rice paper.

When I make the turn onto the switchbacks that climb up the canyon behind Yosemite Falls I run smack into a stiff cold wind funneling down. Zipping up my jacket and pulling my stocking cap down as far as it will go, I push above the six-thousand-foot level, where the scattered snow becomes several inches on the trail. Songs that the French voyageurs sang while canoeing through winter storms on Lake Superior come to mind, and I begin singing because I'm on an adventure battling great odds, or at least dicey weather. I create my own

French-sounding words, since I never knew the original ones and I don't speak French anyway, but I do like to sing loudly when no one can hear me.

At the top of the valley wall everything is hushed at eight thousand feet. Whatever sounds arise are quickly muffled by the foot of snow. The trails heading to both El Cap and North Dome are nowhere to be seen, even through I search for ten minutes. Resigned that this is as far as I go, I wade through the snow toward the creek. The bridge area is a scene of winter beauty, with water running over the gray granite streambed, a sentry of green pine trees, and a brown-beam footbridge. At the fall's overlook I lean over the railing to watch the waterfall flow over the edge and hear little bells ringing. Sierra reindeer? Climbing up the snowy left bank of the river channel and careful not to slip backward and over the canyon wall or to the right into the water and then over the fall, I find a side pool filled with thousands of floating icicles. As Yosemite Creek pulses through, the icicles go up and down, tinkling when they bump each other.

At some point it starts snowing again, the flurries falling quietly into the frozen solitude between Yosemite Point and Eagle Peak and being received by the cupped hands of the river canyon. Although the falls flowing over the edge of the canyon and into the falling snow is pretty enough, the view beyond enchants me: snow settling over hundreds of miles of dark gray mountains. With gray overcast skies above, the starkness of December's black and white colors stretch to the far horizon, where the sun edges the storm with intense bands of yellow and red light. Yosemite's unspoiled wilderness surrounds me and renews my belief in a divine Power. This stunning view from the north rim also unsettles me because of the harshness that governs life in the mountains. Death comes so easily here.

RECENT HISTORY

On March 27, 1851, the Mariposa Battalion stood on the south rim and gazed over the valley before them. Lafayette Bunnell wrote down his amazement. The first tourist party entered the valley four years later. For the first ten years there were about thirty visitors a year, all arriving on horseback. Over the second ten years, attendance increased to an average of one hundred. In 1864, with the guidance of Frederick Olmsted, Yosemite Valley became a state park, released from the federal government by Abraham Lincoln during the Civil War. In 1868, John Muir made his first visit and was smitten. In 1874, the first stagecoach road opened. In 1890, because of the efforts of Muir and Robert Underwood Johnson to stop the sheep that were destroying the natural habitat, Yosemite became a national park.

After an hour enjoying the presence on top of the mountain, I head back down, happy.

In the afternoon I set up a folding chair in the snow of El Capitan's meadow and watch Todd and Jeremy through binoculars as they ply their expertise and courage on El Cap. Stuart is climbing the Cathedral Rocks behind me. A coyote trots by twenty feet away and seems to nod. The slow pace of the climbing and the warmth of the sun on my back lend a sense of eternalness to this hour.

While watching the climbers exposed to the weather I think about the Celts who endured harsh weather on the coast of the North Atlantic. The Celtic people in Scotland were shaped by living on a stone island, fishing a rough, cold sea, and trying to grow crops on green hills that held shallow soil. Under the guidance of

Chief Teneiya, the Ahwahnechees of Yosemite were shaped by oak trees, granite, and waterfalls. They harvested acorns, fished for trout, and traded with neighboring tribes. The Celts sought to be close to nature and understood that the best way to do this was to live simply. Columba of Iona, who hailed from the island off Scotland's western coast, counseled his people to leave all for "the sake of the God of the Elements." Many of his hermits ended up in remote places of great beauty. Even when the Ahwahnechees were removed to a reservation near Fresno, where the weather wasn't as severe, they still tried to return to the valley. Yosemite was like this for John Muir, and perhaps he felt the need for solitude because of his Celtic heritage. With their long history of closeness to nature the Celts have written a vast treasury of nature poems, and today I read their words with newfound appreciation, turning the pages of the book with thick-gloved hands.

After an early dinner of stew I head to my place by the river for the sunset, humming my gratitude with the rest of creation as I walk through the meadow. I'm excited to see my ouzel again on the bend of the river and hear it sing its sweet antiphon. But when I arrive, there is no ouzel. In my disappointment I let go of my expectations and open myself to whatever Yosemite wants to show me instead. Another person joins my solitude along the banks of the river, downstream by the next set of rapids. Unaware of me, she quietly watches the valley, absorbing the rose and yellow alpine colors of the sunset and breathing in the peace settling over the white snow. The valley grows dark as the undulating river flows by and our meditations deepen.

Mariposa Grove

The next afternoon I visit Galen Clark's old cabin and saunter among the giant sequoias of the Mariposa Grove, feeling as close to these trees as if rooted into the earth with them. Clark was the park's first guardian back in the late 1800s. Sitting among the giants I listen to the undisturbed forest filled with the heady aroma of the redwoods. The quiet contemplation of these ancient trees draws me into their corner of the world for an hour to ponder, reflect, and dream.

Nearby the creek gurgles with praise for this day of slower time. I kneel down in the snow and watch one wave flow over a rock and freeze in a clear, thin coat. The next wave melts that, then freezes for a moment before the following wave arrives. This is how our days pass.

I've sought wisdom in the storms and solace in the rivers. At times my adventures have been risky, as when I clung to a tree leaning over the side of a cliff on the Panorama Trail in order to get a better view of the plume of Illilouette Fall—the tree broke off and fell with that section of wall a month later. I've hiked through the backcountry in winter without knowing exactly where the trails actually were. I've walked alone in places that the mountain lions call home. Doing so has taken me beyond where I felt comfortable and placed the fear of death in my mouth. Without challenges like this I would continue to circle around in my little box of understandings. I've had to break through old illusions and undemanding expectations in order to see the vast offerings of nature's beauty and unflinching honesty. This wandering alone has been hard because there is no longer anyone at home to share my adventures.

Camping by myself helped me focus on the wilderness. Yet in talking with Bob and Jason I realize how drawn I was to our conversations, how spending more time with them and others could deepen my understanding and celebration of nature rather than get in the way. Meeting Dana has made me care about dating again, and solitude has given me the time I need to confront my personal demons—impatience, judgmental nature, unfounded fears, and liking stoicism for no discernable reason. I've learned that the wilderness I feared within me isn't so different from what lies inside everyone else.

Evelyn's presence is always with me, especially when I spend time at Happy Isles, her favorite place in the valley. I'm surrounded by the words of John Muir, as well as by owl and hawk, mountain lion and bear, raven and jay, coyote and ouzel, which often show up unexpectedly with surprising inflections of wisdom. I've finally accepted that death is a necessary part of life and that I have had to turn away from home and live in the backcountry of stone for a while to deal with my grief. In spring I think I will be ready to turn back toward life.

When I began this journey I wanted to know why I felt so comfortable in nature. I no longer care about this because I realize that this journey is one that does not end but continues to take me deeper into nature's spirituality. When I return home, Yosemite goes with me. I listen as trees talk in the breeze and I watch as birds fly over. I sit by the few creeks that haven't been covered over in the city and feel in them the flow of the great rivers of earth. When I walk the coastal hills of Point Reyes above the Pacific Ocean, when I hike up Mount Tamalpais from the tranquility of Muir Woods, when I sit by Lake Chabot in the Oakland Hills and look over the Bay Area, I sense the tremendous power of the earth beneath my feet. Nature does not need me to survive, but I need it, and there is so little time to be part of this beauty.

Perhaps in the coming year I will hike on one of the trails that disappear off the edge of the map and just keep walking. Maybe I'll make my introductions to Dana and see where that relationship goes. I am a wanderer now, and one day my molecules, my bits of flesh and bone, will be part of this. This is as life should be, devoured by wonder in mountains of light.

On this Christmas Eve night in 1914, John Muir died. How he loved these trees and wished that he could feel sequoia's pulse, get drunk on sequoia wine, and have sequoia juice run in his veins. The red bark and green branches of the sequoias add a Christmas hue to the snowy landscape. I pick up and cradle three dark-green sequoia cones in my hands. Freshly cut down by Douglas squirrels, the sequoia seeds are tightly bound with the promise of new life to come, seeds that will only sprout after the trauma of a forest fire.

Even the sun is reluctant to set on this glorious day; its colors fade slowly from orange to pink to gray. The evening sky clears of stray clouds and deepens to cobalt blue. Constellations of stars string the sequoia branches with strands of twinkling lights. Then the moon rises, full on this night for the last time for one hundred years. In the distance the whooing of Wawona's owls announce their presence as they begin their protective rounds. Muir was often lonely when hiking through the mountains, yet he realized that this was the only way for him to get close enough to hear nature's voice and feel the power of its spirit. He said that going out into the wilderness was also a journey into the wilderness that lived inside. You were right, John, for both our lives.

I've learned that life only exists in this moment, and it is to this moment that I have to respond as fully as I can, risking everything I have like the climbers in order to keep up with life's changes. The natural world is continuously taking in tragedy and struggle, and recreating that into something new and wonderful. Can I do less?

Back in the valley, I stand in dark Ahwahnee Meadow, unafraid of what wild animals might be around, watching with joy the

warm lights of Curry Village below Glacier Point as they glimmer on the meadow's unbroken snow. On the other side of the
valley the employee cabins nestled under the black protective
cliffs hold people who love this place as much as I do, people who
are singing Jingle Bells to the beat of Native American drums.
Over Half Dome a comet streaks low across the stone mountains
and on into the quiet.

Here in the depths of a winter night, when nature rests in the
solitude of the mountains, I stand on the bank of the Merced
River, the River of Mercy, and listen to the flowing water as it
makes its way to its new home.

Winners of the River Teeth Literary Nonfiction Prize

Five Shades of Shadow
Tracy Daugherty

The Untouched Minutes
Donald Morrill

Where the Trail Grows
Faint: A Year in the Life
of a Therapy Dog Team
Lynne Hugo

The World Before Mirrors
Joan Connor

House of Good Hope:
A Promise for a Broken City
Michael Downs

The Enders Hotel: A Memoir
Brandon R. Schrand

An Inside Passage
Kurt Caswell

Test Ride on the Sunnyland
Bus: A Daughter's Civil Rights
Journey
Ana Maria Spagna

A Double Life: Discovering
Motherhood
Lisa Catherine Harper

Mountains of Light: Seasons of
Reflection in Yosemite
R. Mark Liebenow

To order or obtain more information on these or other University
of Nebraska Press titles, visit www.nebraskapress.unl.edu.